THE PHILOSOPHY OF KING SOLOMON

Colombia para Cristo video introduction

Watch the *La Montaña* trailer, a film based on a true Stendal event

THE PHILOSOPHY OF KING SOLOMON

HIDDEN WISDOM FROM ECCLESIASTES

RUSSELL M. STENDAL

Visit Russell's website: www.cpcsociety.ca

The Philosophy of King Solomon – Russell M. Stendal

First edition published 2016

Cover Design: BookCoverLabs.com

eBook Icon: Icon design/Shutterstock

Editors: Bronwen Jorel and Sheila Wilkinson

Printed in the United States of America

Aneko Press – *Our Readers Matter*™

www.anekopress.com

Life Sentence Publishing, Inc.
203 E. Birch Street
P.O. Box 652
Abbotsford, WI 54405

RELIGION / Biblical Commentary / Old Testament

Paperback ISBN: 978-1-62245-411-2

eBook ISBN: 978-1-62245-412-9

10 9 8 7 6 5 4 3 2 1

Available where books are sold

Share this book on Facebook:

14.95

Contents

For my friends Luciano Marín Arango, Seusis Pausivas Hernández and all of your team.

May your wisdom and understanding surpass that of Solomon.

May you continue to be a blessing to all of our compatriots.

May God bless you and all of our growing number of friends from all backgrounds who genuinely seek and plant peace God's way.

Introduction

For the past three and a half years in my role as a missionary, I have befriended and accompanied many of the men and women who were sent to the city of Havana, Cuba, to negotiate an end to Colombia's fifty-two-year conflict, the longest in the history of this continent. Albert Luepnitz and I, together with other co-workers, felt it imperative to do everything possible to see hearts and minds transformed by the power of the love of God: it's the only real way to stop the killing in Colombia.

Truly this has been a time of intense soul-searching for everyone involved, as agreements have been hammered out for a truth commission, the laying down of weapons, agrarian reform, and a form of transitional justice. These must be acceptable to the international community. Agreeable plans must be made to end the drug traffic, make amends and restitution to the victims, and incorporate the FARC guerrillas back into Colombian society as a peaceful political movement. An all-out attempt to guarantee there will be no repetition of the dreadful things that have happened over the long course of this war is essential.

As Colombia may soon enter this new phase of "post conflict," I feel that it's very important for all of us to consider the following message from the book of Ecclesiastes. King Solomon inherited the ultimate post-conflict opportunity from his father, David. In some ways, Solomon's reign went down in history (approximately 1000 BC) as the golden age of Israel, and yet Solomon, with all his famous wisdom, made some serious mistakes and eventually fell into such terrible apostasy that his kingdom was split and plunged into a death spiral of decline and destruction. (Those who are unfamiliar with this background may read 1 Kings, chapters 1-12 and 2 Chronicles, chapters 1-10.) In this present season of unprecedented political turmoil and conflict, the people of the United States, Israel, the church, and the entire world would also do well to take the lessons of Ecclesiastes to heart.

Brilliant prophetic answers to age-old, philosophical questions and detailed references to God's plan of redemption as it relates to the first and second coming of Jesus Christ are embedded throughout the inspired writings of King Solomon, who lived more than five hundred years before Plato, Socrates, or Aristotle.

At the end of all of our seemingly sublime human accomplishments, will the final verdict be, in the words of Solomon, that everything we have labored for is *vanity of vanities* and *vexation of spirit*?

Chapter One

The Preacher

1 *The words of the Preacher, the son of David, king in Jerusalem.*

Ecclesiastes means "the preacher." He does not choose to identify himself by name in this book, but we know him to have been Solomon.

Later in life, King Solomon, son of King David, became a preacher. He wrote this message in Jerusalem toward the end of his reign. His name means "peace offering." However, while Solomon was undoubtedly *a* son of David, Jesus Christ is the real fulfillment of the peace offering and of all the prophecies about *the* son of David. Under the anointing of the Holy Spirit (for all Scripture is inspired by God), this sermon, written down by Solomon, not only conveys a message to everyone who has lived over the past three millennia, it also contains a deep and detailed message from the heart of God that is prophetic of the end times.

Thirty-three years ago, when I was kidnapped by guerrillas and tied to a tree in the jungles of Colombia for five months, the Lord opened portions of Ecclesiastes to me, as he showed me that this book holds a key message for intellectuals (and for everyone, especially young people) at our present hour. He has added bits and pieces to my understanding of that message over the intervening years. Oswald Chambers has said that it's impossible for us to reason our way out of spiritual confusion; we may only *obey* our way out of confusion. By walking step by step in obedience to God in the midst of many trials and tribulations (and overwhelming grace), I have come to a clearer understanding of this sermon. Truly the blessing of God has overtaken me from behind (Deuteronomy 28:1-2).

What was the preacher preaching?

After phenomenal intellectual and material success, Solomon did not feel fulfilled or satisfied. In the midst of unprecedented riches and prosperity, he was unable to bask in or take delight in his accomplishments.

> 2 *Vanity of vanities, saith the Preacher, vanity of vanities; all is vanity.*
>
> 3 *What profit does a man have of all his labour which he takes under the sun?*
>
> 4 *One generation passes away, and another generation comes, but the earth abides for ever.*
>
> 5 *The sun arises, and the sun goes down, and*

> *with desire returns to his place from which he arises again.*
>
> 6 *The wind goes toward the south and turns about unto the north; it whirls about continually, and the wind returns according to its circuits.*
>
> 7 *All the rivers run into the sea; yet the sea is not full; unto the place from whence the rivers come, there they return again.*
>
> 8 *All things are full of labour; more than man can express; the eye is not satisfied with seeing or the ear filled with hearing.*

The theme of his message is clear from the opening verses.

> 2 *Vanity of vanities, saith the Preacher, vanity of vanities; all is vanity.*

God gave Solomon abundant wisdom and abundant prosperity: prosperity in the things of this world and wisdom in some of the things of God. He acquired much more wealth and influence than any normal person. In fact, he himself stated that it would be very difficult for anyone to repeat what he had done.

Yet, despite all that, he was not satisfied. He sought out new experiences and thereby made grave errors. His worst mistake was that he formed intimate relationships with hundreds of pagan women and eventually joined them in worship of their demonic, bloodthirsty idols. Of course, he had political reasons, but by marrying the women and participating in their worship, he went directly and repeatedly against the word of the Lord.

Then, he concluded that it was all *vanity of vanities*. According to the *American Heritage Dictionary*, *vanity* means "worthlessness, pointlessness, or futility." Describing something as vanity of vanities, then, would have to mean that it was the most worthless, pointless, and futile of all worthless, pointless, and futile things. Solomon asked, perhaps ruefully:

> 3 *What profit does a man have of all his*
> *labour under the sun?*

In Scripture, the sun symbolizes the attraction of this world. Many of the ancients worshipped the sun, but God called such worship an abomination (Ezekiel 8:16-17). The world under the sun is not necessarily submitted to God, and the god (or light) of this world is not the God who created the heavens and the earth. Therefore, every labor of man *under the sun* is a labor of and for this world and will produce nothing of eternal value or profit but only vanity. And despite his many great works and accomplishments that were the wonder of his contemporary world, when Solomon studied the results of all the labor of man *under the sun*, he came to this same conclusion.

Contrast this with Daniel and his three friends who were taken captive and wound up administrating Babylon at the crest of her empire. Scripture doesn't even mention the works that they directed, works of a similar magnitude to those of Solomon. No, the book of Daniel only records what *God* was doing in the midst of the flurry of human activity. What was written in God's book was the wisdom and prophetic revelation that God gave to Daniel.

Solomon recognized that the results of man's labor under the sun were ephemeral and of no intrinsic value. Daniel, however, had a relationship with God that was beyond price.

> 4 *One generation passes away, and another generation comes, but the earth abides for ever.*

In the highest sense, this speaks of the generation of Adam that passes away and the generation of Christ that comes (Matthew 1:1-17; Luke 3:23-37).

Jesus said, *The heaven and the earth shall pass away*, but in Ecclesiastes and elsewhere, Scripture plainly states that the earth abides forever (Matthew 24:35). Jesus said, *Blessed are the meek, for they shall inherit the earth*, and he taught us to pray, *Thy will be done in earth, as it is in heaven* (Matthew 5:5; 6:10). How can those things be true if the earth, and heaven itself, passes away?

Although this seems contradictory, we do something similar when we describe friends and loved ones as having *passed away* when they die. We do not believe that they have ceased to exist, but rather that a transformation has taken place by which their souls have passed into the realm of eternity – either into the presence of God or into the confines of Sheol (Hades in Greek) where they will await their final judgment (2 Corinthians 5:10).

These beliefs about what happens after death were not widely held at the time of Solomon. In fact, at the time of Jesus, the intellectuals known as Sadducees didn't believe in the resurrection or life after death, even though they had the complete canon of the Old Testament (Matthew 22:23). And there are still many "Sadducees" today.

Scripture is clear, however, that the elements of this world will come to an end. When this happens, those who belong to Jesus Christ will be transformed by resurrection and live in a new creation where the heavens and the earth have also been transformed after being judged by fire (Galatians 4:3; 2 Peter 3:10).

The works of man will not survive this judgment. Only the work of God will endure, and God desires to work in us (to cleanse our hearts) and through us (to reach out to others).

Consider, for instance, the magnificent temple that Solomon built. Has the temple itself withstood the ravages of time, or is it instead what the temple symbolized that has endured?

> 5 *The sun arises, and the sun goes down, and with desire returns to his place from which he arises again.*

In this world under the sun, the same basic things happen over and over. Let's look more closely at both the physical and the spiritual aspects of the temple.

In accordance with the plans revealed by God to Solomon's father, David, an outer court contained the altar and a brazen sea that was in the open air *under the sun*. The inner court was the Holy Place of the temple, lit by ten golden lampstands. A veil separated the Holy Place from the Holy of Holies, illuminated not by earthly lampstands but by the glory of the presence of God.

Solomon, even as king of Israel, was not permitted to

enter the Holy Place (let alone the Holy of Holies), where only the priests born of the line of Aaron could minister. During important ceremonies, however, he was allowed to stand next to one of the two pillars located on either side of the porch leading to its entrance. These pillars were thirty-five cubits high, over fifty feet, and the head of each pillar bore a hundred brass pomegranates (symbolizing God's plan by grace for man to bear the fruit of the Spirit). The pillar on the right was named Jachin, "The LORD establishes," and the one on the left was Boaz, "Only in Him is there strength" (2 Chronicles 3:17).

The Holy Place symbolizes the age of grace (the church age) in which there is a priesthood of all born-again believers who minister in the light of the lampstand. The lampstand's sixty-six features of gold symbolize the sixty-six books of the Scriptures, the written Word of God, in the light of the Holy Spirit. Members of this priesthood feed on the showbread, which symbolizes the body of Christ broken for us. They also have access to the throne of God in the Holy of Holies by means of the golden altar of incense, which symbolizes the prayers of the clean people of God. The priests could tend the altar by reaching their hand through the veil.

Even King Solomon was excluded from this realm, as were most others during the age of the Law. He was confined to the outer court *under the sun* of this world. Only those born into the family of Aaron (meaning enlightened) could enter the Holy Place. Now, of course, we may be born again into the life of Jesus Christ and form part of the priesthood of all believers.

And yet God has a replacement for the light of that sun, for he foretold and promised that *unto you that fear my name shall the Sun of righteousness be born* (Malachi 4:2).

The sun of this world cannot bring anything new, but the Sun of righteousness changes everything. In his presence and light, we can have a new beginning and be transformed into new creatures. The fullness of his presence will eventually transform the heavens and the earth (Revelation 20:11; 21:1).

> 6 *The wind goes toward the south and turns about unto the north; it whirls about continually, and the wind returns again according to its circuits.*

The cardinal points of the compass are symbolic. The south is named for the noonday sun and can speak of the maximum expression or favor of the possibilities *under the sun* as they relate to the people of God. The north is named after the cold north wind that can freeze everything and destroy crops. The word for "wind" can be the same as the word for "spirit" and can also be translated as "breath."

The Spirit of God blows upon his people to bless them (the south wind), but at times the "wind" blows from the north and favors those who are apparently not the people of God.

The favor of God blew upon both Israel and the church until, in the midst of prosperity, they became proud and arrogant and turned their backs upon the Lord. Then the wind began to blow in favor of enemies like Babylon from the north, until even a despot like Nebuchadnezzar was deeply touched and converted. The church has gone through similar times.

> 6 *it whirls about continually, and the wind returns again according to its circuits.*

Eventually, in the times and seasons of God, the wind comes back around and blows from the south.

What happened in the New Testament era?

During the age of the church, the wind has blown from all directions, as God, in his wisdom, does not act the way the wise minds of this world would. For instance, the glory of the early church was somehow left behind, and matters reached such a state that the institutional church began to persecute and kill the authentic Christians. Barbarians were at the door, as they burned down Rome. Later, the Vikings were the bane of "Christian" cities of Europe. After successful missionary endeavors, however, the Scandinavian nations became model countries.

And what of the English-speaking world? Over past centuries, the wind of God has blessed western society, but now this society is in deep trouble; the people have turned their backs on God and become cold. This problem has intensified over the past hundred years and continues to accelerate at a breakneck pace.

The entire western-led, world economy is now in serious trouble. Debt is going up on a geometric progression. Central bankers are losing control. World trade agreements, theoretically set up to prevent war and conflict, are instead setting the stage for global conflation.

Why am I saying all of this?

We live in Colombia, a country that has not been a world leader. Much of the news coming from Colombia has been extremely negative. Yet, in the circuit of the wind of the Spirit of God, Colombia has been singled out for greater and greater blessing.

The wind of the Spirit that blew over Great Britain two hundred and fifty years ago and over the United States of America two hundred years ago brought the blessing of God. This blessing, however, has been increasingly taken for granted over the past hundred years by the great English-speaking nations, and the wind of the Spirit has begun to blow from a different direction. Yes, there are still many godly people in the United States, but the nation as a whole is turning its back on God and following its leaders in a different direction.

What would happen if the wind of God were to blow full force upon Colombia and upon the Spanish-speaking world? Can you imagine? Is it even possible?

Indeed it is possible, and it could very well happen, because God is no respecter of persons.

What God did with John Wesley and George Whitefield, what he did in Wales at the turn of the twentieth century, what he did at Azusa Street in 1908, what he did at the 1948 revival in Canada – all this could happen again, this time in a Spanish-speaking environment and with greater world-wide potential.

The year 1967 was one of great prophetic fulfillment, and God did not leave Colombia out. The country began a different spiritual trajectory. After years of confusion and centuries of oppression, in the midst of ever escalating and almost omnipresent corruption, the Spirit of God has blown more and more strongly upon Colombia.

In some of the most unlikely places and under extremely adverse conditions, God is bringing people to maturity in Christ by feeding them with the Word of God. We're beginning to see the results, and we will soon know if what God is doing will be appreciated and acknowledged; we'll find out if the entire nation will change course. Several other Spanish-speaking nations, including Cuba and Venezuela, may soon arrive at a similar crossroads.

We know that the seed of the Word of God needs to fall into good ground, and the only way that there can be good ground is if *we become* the good ground (Matthew 13:8). However, after the fall of man all the ground came under a curse. We can only become good ground if we desire God to remove the curse from us, and he chooses to respond to our prayer.

Once the curse is removed, we will no longer be surrounded by mere vanity in our lives. But the removal of the curse will be painful because it won't leave by magic. It takes cleansing by the fire of God. The curse only leaves our hearts as we allow Father God to discipline us and correct us. We must submit to the dealings of God. If we don't allow his fire to cleanse us, it's impossible to enjoy the fullness of the blessing of God.

Solomon came into great wealth, power, and prosperity without having to suffer first. His father, David, was the one persecuted and purified in the desert prior to receiving the kingdom, and Solomon just stepped into his father's shoes.

However, while David's suffering had been physical in nature, Solomon experienced a different source of sorrow. Even though his name means "peace offering," he was unable to find peace in all the unprecedented wealth, power, and authority that he literally walked into.

He spent most of his life involved in the architecture of great cities, and he lived in unprecedented splendor, only to realize near the end that it was all vanity of vanities. His soul could not find peace in his superb and unsurpassed intellectual knowledge or in all that he ordered and built with his fabulous wealth. Instead, he was plagued with what he describes in Ecclesiastes as *vexation of spirit.*

Peace only stems from a direct link with the presence of the Lord and can only be maintained if we stand in good conscience before God. Fortunately for us, this doesn't mean that if we sin, God washes his hands of us forever, but it does mean that sin and guilt must be dealt with. We must become a living peace offering. It took quite a while for any of this to become clear to Solomon, as he struggled with worldly thoughts and ideas that are common to many intellectuals under the sun.

The way of the cross, the way that Jesus redeemed all of us, is the path that leads to the ultimate peace offering, but only after Jesus' example and sacrifice do the Old Testament lessons and typology really make sense.

As Paul wrote in Romans 11:36, *For of him and by him and in him are all things. To him be the glory for the ages. Amen.*

And a little later, he advised his readers, *Therefore, I beseech you brethren, by the mercies of God, that ye present your bodies in living sacrifice, holy, well pleasing unto God, which is your rational worship. And be not conformed to this age, but be ye transformed by the renewing of your soul that ye may experience what is that good and well pleasing and perfect will of God* (Romans 12:1-2).

> *7 All the rivers run into the sea;*

Scripture compares the gospel to a Word that flows like water.

God's words flow like a river.

In the beginning, the river of God flowed out of Eden and divided into four heads to water the garden (Genesis 2:10). Dew fed the river because at that time rain had never fallen. Without the curse, the entire garden was good earth. (See *The River of God*[1])

At the time of Solomon, as recorded by men like Moses and David, the wisdom of God flowed out of Israel to the *sea* of all the surrounding Gentile nations.

> *7 All the rivers run into the sea; yet the sea is not full;*

God is still directing his river to the sea of lost humanity. Sometimes we can lose patience and, like Solomon, think that all we do is in vain and the Word going forth will have no effect on the sea. Yet the Scripture is clear that the Word of God will not return void (Isaiah 55:11).

> *7 All the rivers run into the sea, yet the sea is not full; unto the place from whence the rivers come, there they return again.*

1 Russell Stendal, *The River of God* (Abbotsford, Wis.: ANEKO Press, 2014).

Even without the help of modern science, Solomon knew that all the water from all the rivers flows into the sea and must eventually return to its source and continue to flow.

The Word of God continues to flow and flow until it causes the desired effect. Man can contaminate the rivers, but the rivers reach the sea nonetheless. This Word of God is for those who choose to respond to his call.

The only way for the word or the water to return to its source is by changing its state. The only way water can return to the mountains from whence it came is by becoming pure water vapor. In Solomon's time, however, this part of the cycle was a complete mystery.

Jesus is the living Word of God. He was sent from on high, became flesh, and died for all of us who are struggling to stay afloat in the lost sea of humanity. He did this so we might be able to receive the life of God by the Spirit. After changing his state from life to death to life again, Jesus returned to the Father from whence he came, having accomplished the work of redemption. The Word sent by the Father did not return void.

Much, much more could be said about the cycle of the rivers that flow into the sea and the way this image parallels God's Word. Sometimes the water is frozen and locked in ice caps or glaciers for thousands of years, waiting for the time when the ice will melt and the waters will be released. Similarly, some of the things God said thousands of years ago appear to be "frozen," but they will all be released in the proper season. In the book of Revelation, for example, we learn of seven golden vials of the wrath of God that contain accumulated prayers from God's people over millennia, and we understand that one day, at the end of the world as we know it, this wrath will suddenly be poured out and released as judgments of God (Revelation 5:8; 15:7).

There is a word that flows first upon the "land" (the people of God) and eventually reaches the sea of lost humanity. In the land of Israel, the Jordan River flows into the Dead Sea, so named because the minerals and contaminants are so concentrated in it that no fish or other complex marine life can survive. The limited amount of incoming water from the Jordan can't change this deadly balance. *Jordan* means "flowing down" and symbolizes death.

God promises to change the river of death into a pure river of the water of life, clear as crystal, proceeding out of the throne of God and of the Lamb (Revelation 22:1). When this happens, there will be no more sea (Revelation 21:1); there will no longer be any sea of lost humanity.

As God's Word continues to flow into the sea, those who do not wish to respond will be free to make that choice, but life will continue to flow from the presence of God in and through the lives of all those who respond to him, until his will is fully accomplished.

Places like Colombia, which in times past had little opportunity to receive the clean word of the Lord, will have that opportunity in abundance. In North America, the Pilgrim fathers brought their faith with them. In South America, however, the land was conquered by brutal, bloodthirsty Spanish conquistadors, emptied out of the prisons of Spain with the Spanish Inquisition close upon their heels. They sought riches and women and slaves, not freedom of religious expression. Nevertheless, God's purpose will not be denied. The rivers of his Word will continue to flow into the sea until those purposes are fully accomplished, and the Spanish-speaking world will be no exception.

God is granting a new opportunity for waters that were once part of the contaminated sea of lost humanity to undergo a purifying change of state. Those who seize this opportunity will enter into his plan and purpose by the Spirit. God will fill each of these souls with his presence and saturate them with his Word. Then he will send them forth, carrying the precious gift of the clean water of the Word into the arid, sterile desert of the religion and politics and economics controlled by man and into the sea of those who are lost.

> 8 *All things are full of labour; more than man can express; the eye is not satisfied with seeing nor the ear filled with hearing.*

The work or labor of man is complicated. For some, there is seemingly endless drudgery. For others, new knowledge and technological advances do not seem to bring lasting peace and satisfaction. The same old grind continues. There is literally no end of things to see and hear.

Jesus spoke to those who, by the Spirit, had *ears to hear* and *eyes to see* what God is saying and doing.

> 9 *The thing that has been, it is that which shall be; and that which is done is that which shall be done; and there is no new thing under the sun.*

Man seems unable to learn from the mistakes of the past.

We are told that those who fail to learn from history are doomed to repeat it, and this is undoubtedly true. There is no new thing under the sun, only various repetitions of the past.

God, however, has a new sun, the Sun of Righteousness, with healing in his wings that will even lead to *new heavens and a new earth* (Isaiah 65:17; Isaiah 66:22; 2 Peter 3:13).

> 10 *Is there any thing of which it may be said, See, this is new? it has been already of old time which was before us.*

I believe that in the context of his message Solomon is referring to intellectual accomplishments and not to technology. The thinking of the natural man cannot escape the past.

> 11 *There is no remembrance of former things; neither shall there be any remembrance of things that are to come with those that shall come after.*

This is what Solomon thought. There have been and still are many intellectuals like him, who view life as short lived and find neither point nor value in anything.

> 12 *I the Preacher was king over Israel in Jerusalem.*

> 13 *And I gave my heart to seek and search out by wisdom concerning all things that are done under heaven (this sore travail God has given to the sons of man that they be occupied in it).*

How many preachers have seated themselves as kings over the people of God here upon the earth?
And what have those "kings" given their hearts over to? They will tell you that they, like Solomon, have devoted their hearts *to seek and search out by wisdom* and to make inquisition. How many books – how many libraries – are filled with the works of persons like this? And what, ultimately, are all those thousands of words worth?

Solomon at least realized at the beginning of his book that on a human level, all of his wisdom and learning and accomplishments were only *vanity of vanities.*

> 14 *I have seen all the works that are done under the sun; and, behold, all is vanity and vexation of spirit.*

Those who are busily building up their own kingdoms in the name of God, those who are founding institutions in the name of God, and those who are twisting arms and taking up offerings, making their own headquarters and developing franchises in the name of God, all claim one thing:

That it is all for God, and they are merely servants or administrators. They would have us believe that the wealth and power they accumulate is only a fortunate by-product.

In terms of wealth and power, Solomon had much more than any of them. He had a temple built from plans that God himself had given his father, David. More resources were spent on this temple than most prosperity preachers can even conceive of today. Yet who among such preachers is willing to consider the wise advice of Solomon?

> 14 *I have seen all the works that are done under the sun; and, behold, all is vanity and vexation of spirit.*

What about all the things that we do on our own account in the name of God?

We may readily see when some church leaders go wrong, but if we look honestly at our own behavior, how do we measure up? Are we putting our time to its best use? Unless we desist from all of this vanity and vexation of spirit, it is difficult for the Lord to work in and through us.

Solomon's descendants formed a long line of kings, and Scripture states that some of them set their hearts to follow God and some did not. None of them, however, quit doing things on their own. It all came to a sad end called the Babylonian captivity. (*Babylon* means "confusion.")

> 15 *That which is crooked cannot be made straight, and that which is lacking cannot be numbered.*

Solomon argues that the nature of Adam cannot be straightened out, or in other words, the old man cannot be rehabilitated because something intangible will always be lacking. The natural man isn't even aware of all that has been lost as the human race continues to degenerate.

Those who use gifts and ministries from God to seek personal gain and the prosperity of this world believe that the crooked cannot be made straight. They may publicly "confess" their sins in a show of repentance, but they never seem to truly repent. Repentance requires a complete course reversal, which is beyond their powers if they leave God out of the equation and rely only on themselves. Since they find that they cannot walk in victory over the flesh, over the world, or over the Devil, they believe that it's impossible. They don't believe that the human heart can attain to perfection. This is true of all those who spiritually remain in the "outer court of the temple" under the sun.

Their message could be summed up as: "Join us in doing great and wonderful works here upon the earth and this will ease your guilt. You feel guilty because you are a member of mankind, and man is doomed to sin in word, thought, and deed, as well as by omission. Come and confess your sins on a daily basis, pay your tithes, and attend endless religious rites and rituals. These obligations will never end, because that which is twisted cannot be straightened, and there is nothing new under the sun."

The light of the wisdom of this world is like this, but the Lord says that his new day can begin within us. He tells us that before the promised new day with the coming Sun of righteousness, the Morning Star can shine and illuminate each of our hearts with the light and the sustained presence of Jesus Christ (Proverbs 4:18; 2 Peter 1:19). Rivers of the water of life will begin to flow from our innermost being into the spiritual desert around us. When we become part of the new man in Christ, the old rules about what happens under the sun of this world no longer apply. This is the beginning of the *new thing* that

Isaiah prophesied: *Behold, I will do a new thing; it shall come to light quickly; shall ye not know it? I will again make a way in the wilderness and rivers in the desert* (Isaiah 43:19).

> 16 *I communed with my own heart, saying, Behold, I am come to great estate and have gotten more wisdom than all those that have been before me in Jerusalem; and my heart had great experience of wisdom and knowledge.*

Solomon's way was not the way of his father, David, much less the way of Jesus Christ, who said that the greatest in the kingdom of God is the least important servant of all, and the humble will be exalted.

> 17 *And I gave my heart to know wisdom and knowledge and to know folly and those who are mad; I learned in the end that this also is vexation of spirit.*

I wonder: Do the great prosperity preachers who claim to have the largest, greatest churches and who profess to be the apostles over everyone else because they excel in wisdom and knowledge also excel in folly and madness?

From my own observations, I would say that they seem unable even to contain, let alone desist from, their folly and madness. We all know what folly is, and madness is used here in the sense of lunacy or craziness. A little leaven of either of these conditions soon leavens the entire lump.

Those who focus on their own heart will never be able to escape folly and madness. They will always place themselves (and their group, ministry, denomination, or political affiliation) at the center of their universe. Those who have the heart of Jesus, however, realize that *he* is the center of the universe.

God's plan is not to rehabilitate the fallen nature of Adam in each of us. God's plan is not to equip our Adamic nature with great wisdom and profound knowledge of our human condition. Rather, God's plan is for the old man to die so that by the Spirit of God, Jesus Christ can live and reign in each of our hearts.

Solomon failed to understand this until it was almost too late. Near the end of his life, when this book was written, all his earlier hard work was lost, and he saw that everything was vanity of vanities. Solomon appears to have been saved with little or nothing (in terms of heavenly treasure) to show for having lived. He lacked the proper foundation for his life. *For no one can lay another foundation than that laid, which is Jesus the Christ. Now if anyone builds upon this foundation gold, silver, precious stones, wood, hay, stubble, the work of each one shall be made manifest, for the day shall declare it because it shall be revealed by fire; the work of each one, whatever sort it is, the fire shall put it to test. If the work of anyone abides which he has built thereupon, he shall receive a reward. If anyone's work shall be burned, he shall suffer loss, but he himself shall be saved, yet so as by fire* (1 Corinthians 3:11-15).

God desires that intellectuals and those who seek the prosperity of this world should be saved. In order for this to happen, however, at a bare minimum they must be standing on the right foundation (which is Jesus Christ, not humanism). It would be very sad if, despite their wisdom and wealth, these people were saved so as by fire, like Solomon. Listen to the Preacher's words:

> 18 *For in much wisdom is much grief, and he that increases knowledge increases sorrow.*

Think of the many institutes of theology and higher learning where the joy of the Holy Spirit fails to flow and where the student body and faculty seem to fit this picture of grief and sorrow. In these places, success seems to be measured by the elements of this corrupt world. Both teachers and students appear to think that if they are successful by worldly standards, God must be blessing them. Even those who pride themselves on not coveting personal gain may delight in all the trappings of the great religious and secular empires that they help to construct.

Those who place themselves under the mighty hand of God to receive his correction may in the beginning not seem to prosper according to the way this world measures success. Things may tighten up for them financially until the Lord cleanses their hearts. Even when they have clean hearts and God begins to bless and give them resources, things may remain tight.

Do you know why?

When a person with a heart for God receives more of the things of this world, they will also have a much greater perception of the problems and needs of those around them. Their hearts will feel the pain of those who are in trouble, and as they *have* more and more, they will *share* more and more. They will choose to continue living on a tight budget, so they can invest in heavenly treasure. God notices this.

We must learn to depend on each word that proceeds from the mouth of God (Deuteronomy 8:3; Matthew 4:4). It's the only way.

The Lord is close to instituting radical change. He will soon bring down the kingdoms of this world, because *his* kingdom operates on an entirely different basis. Every kingdom built by man will ultimately fall.

Let us pray

Heavenly Father,
May we learn from the mistakes of others so we do not continue in the same error. May we be cut free from the tentacles of this world under the sun, so we may be fed and illuminated by your living Word. Amen.

Chapter Two

Vanity and Vexation of Spirit

Solomon received a tremendous inheritance from David, his father. He was chosen by God to build the temple. His kingdom was known as the golden age of Israel. No king before or after even came close to his natural wisdom or wealth. But look at what he records here:

> 1 *I said in my heart, Come now, I will prove thee with mirth, therefore enjoy good things; and, behold, this also is vanity.*
>
> 2 *I said of laughter, It is mad, and of mirth, What does it do?*
>
> 3 *I proposed in my heart to regale my flesh with wine and that my heart would walk in wisdom; and to lay hold on folly, until I might see what was that good for the sons of men, which they should do under the heaven all the days of their life.*

4 *I made myself great works; I built myself houses; I planted myself vineyards;*

5 *I made myself gardens and orchards, and I planted trees in them of all kind of fruits;*

6 *I made myself pools of water, to water with them the forest that brings forth trees;*

7 *I got myself slaves and maidens and had sons born in my house; also I had great possessions of cattle and sheep above all that were in Jerusalem before me;*

8 *I gathered unto myself also silver and gold and the peculiar treasure of kings and of the provinces; I obtained men singers and women singers and all the delights of the sons of men, musical instruments, and those of all sorts.*

9 *So I was great and increased more than all that were before me in Jerusalem, and more than that, my wisdom remained with me.*

10 *And whatever my eyes desired I did not keep from them; I did not withhold my heart from any pleasure; for my heart rejoiced in all my labour, and this was my portion of all my labour.*

11 *At last I looked on all the works that my hands had wrought and on the labour that I had laboured to do; and, behold, all was*

vanity and vexation of spirit, and there was no profit under the sun.

King David passed through many trials and tribulations. He fought many difficult battles. Solomon, on the other hand, received the kingdom in peace. He knew no war. He had the talent and the money to indulge himself with the kind of creativity he describes in the verses above. Some of his works have probably not been equaled even today.

However, Solomon is also a symbol of another time and age.

Never in the history of the world has there been a time of prosperity as great as that which has been enjoyed by the western world in general and the United States in particular. In the religious world, the works that man has made in the name of God are above and beyond any previous accomplishment. We've built not only immense cathedrals, temples, and mosques, but also giant evangelical church fortresses.

When in history has the like been seen?

Churches have their own fleet of busses to bring in the people, ushers with credit card processors patrolling the aisles, ATM machines and fast food coffee shops in the foyer, and amusement parks for the children and young people under the same roof. Every type of religious commerce is available, including fashion shows, world travel tours, books, movies, CDs, DVDs, retirement plans, even funeral plans. In some areas we've outdone even Solomon. What would he say if he could see all that we have done? We may get a clue if we consider:

What does Solomon say about all the over-the-top things that he accomplished?

> 11b *Behold, all was vanity and vexation of spirit, and there was no profit under the sun.*

Even with all the blessings that God can shower upon us, prosperity continues to be a much greater test than adversity. As recorded in Scripture, the vast majority of the people of God rapidly turned away from him when enjoying prosperity and only returned to him in times of great adversity.

How is Colombia doing in this regard?

The great Colombian cities are similar in many ways to the cities of the United States. Some of the large Colombian churches are splurging on the same excesses as their counterparts in North America.

Yet where there is trouble, where things are tight, where life is not easy, many people are open to the Lord, and he is awakening them spiritually.

The Scripture is clear: all the sleeping virgins, both the wise and the foolish, will be awakened when the bridegroom arrives, but only the wise will be prepared (Matthew 25:5-12). Bear in mind that in Bible prophecy, women can represent entire congregations or even denominations.

While it is true that the foolish ones will also awaken before the end, for many of them, unfortunately, when they finally wake up, it will be too late for them to establish a connection to the source of the oil (the anointing of an intimate relationship with God) that is necessary to prevent their lamps from going out.

There is another aspect to this most important lesson:
In the midst of their participation in the unprecedented material prosperity of the world around them, many think that their success in obtaining the things of this world is the equivalent to God's seal of approval upon them and upon their behavior. This is not necessarily the case. When God miraculously blesses and prospers us as individuals or in ministry, he is primarily making a statement about himself and who he is and not necessarily endorsing us.

My friend Clayt Sonmore said that one of the worst judgments that can befall God's people is to have God grant their requests when they ask amiss. Solomon finally discovered this. Sadly, by the time he came to his senses, the seeds that would result in the fracture of the kingdom of Israel were already sown. Prosperity accelerates the tendency for the splits and divisions that are the bane of the modern-day church, whereas in times of persecution and adversity, God's people tend to stick together. In line with this principle, Israel and Judah split at what appeared to be the pinnacle of their golden age.

In the book of Revelation, the Lord dictated seven letters that were addressed to seven congregations but applicable to all the churches. The first six letters are addressed to *the angel of the congregation in or of*, followed by the name of a particular city, but the seventh is uniquely addressed to *the angel of the congregation of the* ***Laodiceans***, suggesting that they considered it to be *their* church rather than Christ's church in or of

Laodicea. Jesus is depicted as standing outside calling to see if they would let him back in (Revelation 3:14-20). This is applicable to many churches (or congregations) that have gone head over heels into the prosperity of the things of this world instead of seeking first the kingdom of God and his righteousness (Matthew 6:33).

> 12 *And I turned myself to behold wisdom and those who are mad, and folly; for what can the man do that comes after the king? even that which has already been done.*

In order to behold wisdom and see who the real lunatics were, Solomon had to turn himself away from contemplating all the seemingly wonderful things of this world that he had acquired or caused to be created. He had mobilized the entire nation to accomplish what he thought were great works for God, only to find in the end that much of this work turned out to have been folly.

Solomon covered the entire nation in beautiful, immense, elegant sites that make the Vatican pale by comparison. The amount of gold used for his temple may well have been more than that stored in Fort Knox at the height of the gold standard. David had gathered vast riches during the victorious wars by which he subjugated all the surrounding nations. The pagans had spent centuries gathering all the gold they could get their hands on and storing it before their idols. David captured it and dedicated it for Solomon's temple.

The ongoing yearly tribute that came in from abroad to Solomon was 666 talents of gold per year, which was a fabulous sum (2 Chronicles 9:13). Six is a number related to man. Six hundred can mean man's plans. Ten refers to the law. Sixty can mean man's laws. The number one relates to light. Six can mean man's light. When the situation is not fully submitted to God, 666 signifies man's plans according to man's laws in the humanistic light of man. This number is associated with the mark and name of the beast. This mark must be placed in the right hand or in the forehead of those who worship the image of the beast (Revelation 13:16-18). The mark has to do with the way of acting and thinking of the natural man, who is really a beast.

> 13 *And I have seen that wisdom excels folly as far as light excels darkness.*

> 14 *The wise man has eyes in his head, but the fool walks in darkness: And I myself also understood that one event happens to one and to the other.*

Regardless of what we obtain or accomplish in this life, either for good or for evil, we are all destined to die and afterward to be judged (Hebrews 9:27).

> 15 *Then I said in my heart, As it shall happen to the fool, so it shall happen even to me. Why have I worked until now to make myself wiser? Then I said in my heart that this also is vanity.*

How much wiser can we make ourselves?

> 16 *For there is no remembrance of the wise more than of the fool for ever, seeing that which now is in the days to come shall all be*

forgotten. And also the wise man shall die the same as the fool.

17 *Therefore I hated life because every work that is wrought under the sun was grievous unto me; for all was vanity and vexation of spirit.*

Solomon was not paying attention when his father, David, spent hours or days on end in direct communion with God before the ark of the covenant. The plans for the temple were revealed to David as he contemplated the beauty of the Lord (Psalm 27:4).

Solomon apparently did not contemplate the beauty of the Lord, he received no invitation from God to enter the realm of the ark of God; he simply received the temple plans that his father left him. He did not really believe David's written reminder that the fear of the Lord is the beginning of wisdom and that he should guard his heart above all else.

When Solomon finished the temple and the sanctified priests placed the ark of the covenant inside, the glory of God filled the temple with such intensity that no one could enter to minister (2 Chronicles 7:2). Solomon also remained outside. To enter the glory of God would have cost him his own life, but he could have discovered a new sun, the Sun of righteousness. He could have entered into the realm of the new creation where everything is made new.

18 *Yea, I hated all my labour which I had taken under the sun, which I should leave it unto the man that shall be after me.*

Solomon has realized that remaining in the natural realm is futile and ultimately fatal. Many talented and creative people have come to the same conclusion. Some have even committed suicide in their despair.

With all his supposed wisdom, Solomon had been following the wrong path. Many of his labors had gone directly against the word of the Lord.

For example, God had told the kings of Israel that they should not return to Egypt to multiply horses unto themselves; they were not to multiply wives unto themselves; they were not even to multiply silver or gold unto themselves (Deuteronomy 17:14-20).

Solomon started on the wrong path with Pharaoh's daughter and went on to not only acquire a thousand women but even to build shrines, temples, and high places to their pagan demonic gods. These buildings were a stumbling block in Israel for more than four hundred years.

God instructed the kings of Israel not to trust in iron chariots or in horses, yet Solomon built stables for thousands of horses and had hundreds of iron chariots. He even supplied horses and chariots from Egypt to most of his neighbors.

None of this brought him true satisfaction though, and he finally asked what should it profit a man if he gains the entire world and loses his soul?

> 18 *Yea, I hated all my labour which I had taken under the sun, which I should leave it unto the man that shall be after me.*
>
> 19 *And who knows whether he shall be a wise man or a fool, he who shall have rule over*

all my labour in which I have labored and in which I have showed myself wise under the sun? This is also vanity.

Many talented leaders reach the same conclusion. After years of putting together a giant consortium, acquiring millions of dollars, and spending their genius organizing and controlling a great empire, they ask the same questions that Solomon did. Who will be the heir? Will the heir turn out to be a wise successor or foolish one? What will happen to the empire when the founder is gone? What will be the eternal value of all the founder's hard labor?

In Christian terms, what is the eternal value of congregating large multitudes and building bigger and better headquarters if no viable fruit of righteousness is being produced because the people are not really coming to maturity in Christ?

These leaders have been telling people who desire earthly riches that if they sacrificially give money to the institution that has been set up, God will multiply it a hundredfold. Or they have been laying guilt trips on the people by describing the poor, needy, oppressed, and persecuted souls that their ministry specializes in helping or evangelizing, when in fact the lion's share of their budget goes into paying professional fund raisers to raise ever more money and sustaining a large headquarters full of media professionals.

On the other hand, if the leaders were to ask, "Who wants to be a martyr for the cause of the gospel?" far fewer would respond positively.

20 *Therefore my heart began to despair again*

regarding all the labour which I took under the sun.

Working under the sun of this world is one thing and can indeed lead to despair. Working for the Sun of righteousness is quite another and can lead to joy beyond measure.

21 *That the man who worked with wisdom and with knowledge and with uprightness would have to leave his portion to a man that has not laboured therein. This also is vanity and a great evil.*

Solomon continues to have a high opinion of himself, bolstered by his unprecedented success under the sun. He remains convinced that he has done all of this honestly with great wisdom and knowledge and uprightness. He is blind to the consequences of all the women, horses, chariots, gold, and silver that he acquired contrary to the will of God. He continues to think that all the great works that he has accomplished should be secured for all posterity. He is sure that it would be vanity and a great evil to leave all of this to someone who did not have to work for it the way he did.

The modern-day equivalent to all of this is congregations, franchises, and religious and secular machinery in general (iron chariots), pulled by horses (by people operating in the flesh).

If Solomon's temple ended up as rubble with not even one stone on top of another, what fate awaits the Vatican? And what about all of the smaller Vaticans that abound?

Into whose hands will they fall, and what will be the power plays and intrigue? How long will they endure?

Prosperity of this world in such magnitude (even in the name of the Lord) is a sitting duck for those who would like to make a hostile takeover. If this is not possible, there will always be those looking to take a piece at a time, usually surreptitiously.

Instead of shepherds (pastors) willing to give their lives for the sheep, some are expert at fleecing the sheep. In many places the wolves are full-time staff members. For all his high opinion of himself, Solomon was now having second thoughts about how he spent his time and the resources of his kingdom. Was it really worthwhile, he asks, to labor and build and amass all this when it's all transient and there's no one who is even worthy to inherit it?

If we spend our time as true servants of the Lord and of his people and God changes each heart, these people begin to produce the fruit of righteousness, as they begin to express the character of God. The love of God will flow by the Spirit and keep on flowing. No one can ever suppress it or take it away. We will have no worldly legacy to worry about, but all the results will go directly into God's heavenly barn and there will never be a loss.

In worldly terms, who could possibly aspire to have more than Solomon? No one. Yet Solomon described everything he labored for as vanity and affliction of spirit.

This is a lesson that most have yet to learn.

> 22 *For what does man have of all his labour and of the vexation of his heart in which he has laboured under the sun?*

Scripture is clear that only the work accomplished by God is eternal.

The Lord is still knocking at the door of the hearts and the corporate institutions of his people, hoping they will open the door so he can purify their hearts and correct the root of their problem.

If we allow the Lord to work in our hearts and conform them to his desires, he can work through us, and the results are eternal. He can multiply his life and touch others.

When man in his wisdom (under the sun) does things backwards, however, look what happens:

> 23 *For all his days are only sorrows, and his travail grief; yea, his heart does not take rest in the night. This also is vanity.*
>
> 24 *There is nothing better for a man than that he should eat and drink and that he should make his soul enjoy good in his labour. I also have seen that this is from the hand of God.*

The only work that is worthwhile relates to the hand of God. God desires to place his hand on us. He may have to bring us to the sad realization that everything we have done apart from him is vanity, but when we comprehend this fact, we are free to understand that only the food and drink provided by Father God can truly sustain and satisfy us.

> 25 *For who can eat and who can care for himself better than I?*

Jesus said, *Blessed are those who hunger and thirst for*

righteousness, for they shall be satisfied (Matthew 5:6). This may be the reason that he also said, *Behold, a greater than Solomon is here* (Matthew 12:42).

> 26 *For God gives to the man that is good in his sight wisdom and knowledge and joy, but to the sinner he gives travail, to gather and to heap up, that he may give to the one that is good before God. This also is vanity and vexation of spirit.*

Even after being given – perhaps especially after being given – the management of all the riches that his father, David, captured from all the pagan empires, Solomon had difficulty understanding the real reason that we are here even though God gave him great wisdom *under the sun*. Only late in his life after he had spent most of his years planting the wrong crop, did he understand.

All of Solomon's follies are written down in the book of Kings (likely accumulated by scribes). It is interesting to note, however, that his apostasy is not recorded in the book of Chronicles (likely written by prophets or by priests at the temple). These two accounts are in the Scriptures yet written from different points of view. David's sin is not listed in the book of Chronicles either, but the sin of Saul, his predecessor, is.

Solomon came out clean in the book of Chronicles because when God forgives, he doesn't remember our sins and trespasses. But even though it appears that Solomon was saved in the end, the Kingdom of Israel was divided and gradually went from bad to worse after his death.

Where are the works of Solomon now?

The fate of the ark of the covenant is not even known. It was last mentioned about the time of the visit of the Queen of Sheba, when Solomon is on record as having given her whatever she desired. Similarly, nothing is left of Solomon's temple even after it was rebuilt on at least two occasions.

I don't think we could have a better example of why not to place our attention and focus on the things of this world. Jesus said that if we seek first the kingdom of God and his righteousness, all these things would be added unto us. If we follow Jesus' advice, we can avoid the path of vanity, affliction of spirit, and all that Solomon suffered in the midst of the greatest worldly prosperity imaginable.

Jesus said that our heart will be where our treasure is. We have the opportunity – if the Spirit leads us – to invest our time and resources in things that have eternal value.

Let us pray

Lord,
We thank you for the fact that we are alive today and for the opportunities that we have been given to invest our time and resources wisely, according to the leading of your Spirit, so at your return we may be found doing your will. Amen.

Chapter Three

A Time for Everything

1 *For all things there is a season, and every will under the heaven has its time determined.*

2 *A time to be born, and a time to die; a time to plant, and a time to pluck up that which is planted;*

3 *a time to kill, and a time to heal; a time to break down, and a time to build up;*

4 *a time to weep, and a time to laugh; a time to mourn, and a time to dance;*

5 *a time to cast away stones, and a time to gather stones together; a time to embrace, and a time to refrain from embracing;*

6 *a time to seek, and a time to lose; a time to keep, and a time to cast away;*

7 *a time to rend, and a time to sew; a time to keep silence, and a time to speak;*

8 *a time to love, and a time to hate; a time of war, and a time of peace.*

The words describe our lives on earth, where all things have their time or season. As human beings, we can all expect to have our share of joy and sorrow, safety and peril, love and loneliness. But what of our spiritual lives?

> 1 *For all things there is a season, and every will under the heaven has its time determined.*

Every person *under the heaven* has a will of their own. The Devil certainly had a will of his own, and what he desired was to replace God. This was his thought when he instigated the fall of Adam and Eve, so they would not have dominion over him. With the rebellion of the third part of the angels who followed him, Satan thought he would be able to prevail in heaven, but this was not to be. Every will *under* heaven has its time determined, and Satan and his angels will soon be cast out of heaven into the earth (Revelation 12:9).

> 2 *A time to be born, and a time to die; a time to plant, and a time to pluck up that which is planted;*

If the Devil had known what God knows, he probably wouldn't have done what he did. Under the heaven, there is *a time to be born and a time to die*. The Devil didn't have a clue as to how this would apply to the plan of God for the redemption of mankind.

Jesus left heaven, was born on earth as a man, and voluntarily gave his life for us. That he would do this is completely foreign to how the Devil thinks. Jesus also described himself as a seed that would fall into the ground (be planted) and die so it could be multiplied. This is how

God decided to multiply the quality of the life of Jesus into people like us.

Look at the consequences that the Devil did not consider:

He never thought that Jesus would become a man and die. And when he saw that Jesus was on earth, the Devil attempted to kill him (or have him killed) to be able to hold him in Hades by death. Jesus, however, broke the power of death and took the keys of Hades and of death away from Satan (Revelation 1:18).

It is possible to die as a consequence of disobedience, sin, or rebellion, but Jesus was innocent of all three and died in obedience to his Father; through his obedience he overcame death. Jesus' death and resurrection opened the way for him to send us the Holy Spirit that we might walk in his victory. By the Spirit, we may put to death the deeds of the flesh and live (Romans 8:13). By the Spirit, reconciled with God by Jesus' death, all the evils that the Devil planted in us can be plucked out, no matter how deep their roots may have grown.

> 3 *a time to kill, and a time to heal; a time to break down, and a time to build up;*

Jesus submitted to death so we might be healed. God's plan is to kill the old man (old nature) that we are born with and heal (restore) our souls with the life of Christ (Psalm 23:3). This deals a mortal blow to Satan's kingdom of darkness. As the work of the Devil is broken down, the kingdom of God is built up.

> 4 *a time to weep, and a time to laugh; a time to mourn, and a time to dance;*

Jesus said, *Blessed are those that weep now, for ye shall laugh* (Luke 6:21), and *Blessed are those that mourn, for they shall be comforted* (Matthew 5:4). If we suffer with Christ, we shall reign with him. If we allow God to deal with our fallen human nature, we may initially mourn, but we shall be comforted by the Holy Spirit, and joy will return to our lives. Remember the prodigal son? He had fallen low, but when he repented and returned home, music and dancing were soon heard in the house (Luke 15:25).

> 5 *a time to cast away stones, and a time to gather stones together; a time to embrace, and a time to refrain from embracing;*

According to the word of Jesus, all of the stones of Solomon's temple would eventually be cast down until not one remained on top of another (Matthew 24:1-2). Later, Jesus promised to make those who follow him into living stones, as part of an everlasting temple not made with hands (1 Peter 2:5). If we truly embrace Jesus, we must also be willing to cast away everything that he doesn't like in our lives.

> 6 *a time to seek, and a time to lose; a time to keep, and a time to cast away;*

Now we are commissioned to seek the lost. We are encouraged to lose our own lives so we may discover our existence in Him. We will keep the wisdom from above and cast away our folly.

> *7 a time to rend, and a time to sew; a time to keep silence, and a time to speak;*

God told Solomon that he would rend the kingdom from him because he had not kept God's covenant and his statutes (1 Kings 11:11). When we are given a warning as serious as this, God tells us to *rend your heart, and not your garments, and turn unto the LORD your God for he is gracious and compassionate, slow to anger and great in mercy, and he does repent of chastisement* (Joel 2:13). Job said that he had sewn sackcloth upon his flesh in a symbol of repentance (Job 16:15). When Job ran out of words and kept silent, however, God spoke and revealed himself (Job 31:40; 38:1; 42:1-6).

> *8 a time to love, and a time to hate; a time of war, and a time of peace.*

The Lord Jesus loved us first. Now he desires for us to love God and one another. In order to do this, we must have a change of heart. When the love of God flows in our hearts, we will also hate the evil that God hates.

Therefore, as we learn to overcome evil with good by the Spirit, there is a time of war followed by a time of peace. True peace flows from the presence and power of God.

> *9 What profit does the one that works have in that which he labours?*

What will our own good works profit us?

What did Solomon's great works profit him? We know from his own words that Solomon's great works proved hollow and vain. However, if we allow the Lord to do his work in and through us, the results of our works will be different. Our own works, even with the best intentions, will only be temporal, but his work in and through us is eternal.

To which type of work will we dedicate our time and resources?

> 10 *I have seen the travail which God has given to the sons of men that they may be occupied in it.*

Solomon knew about travail. Not that he performed labor himself, of course. Instead, *Solomon counted seventy thousand men to bear burdens and eighty thousand to hew in the mountain, and three thousand six hundred to oversee them* (2 Chronicles 2:2). Solomon used forced labor to build the temple. But Jesus said: *My yoke is easy and my burden is light* (Matthew 11:30).

As Paul wrote to the Ephesians, *For we are his workmanship, created in Christ Jesus for good works, which God has prepared that we should walk in them* (Ephesians 2:10). The good works prepared by God for us to walk in will produce eternal results such as the fruit of the Holy Spirit (Galatians 5:22-23; Ephesians 5:9-10). The Lord can then multiply this because the seed is in the fruit.

> 11 *He has made everything beautiful in his time: even the world he has given over to their will, in such a way that no man can attain to this work that God makes from the beginning to the end.*

The world is given over to the will of man, yet there is no

comparison between the accomplishments of the world of men and the creative work of God.

> 12 *I have learned that there is nothing better for them, but to rejoice and to do good in his life.*

The only way for us to truly do good is in his life – in the life of God. This is the only way we will ever be fulfilled and satisfied and the only way we will ever be able to rejoice spontaneously.

> 13 *And also that every man should eat and drink and enjoy the good of all his labour; it is the gift of God.*

The Scripture states that man shall not live by bread alone but by every word that proceeds from the mouth of God (Deuteronomy 8:3; Luke 4:4).

How can we enjoy the good of all our labor?

Only by being in the will of God. Otherwise, like Solomon, we will eventually discover that all is vanity, vexation of spirit, and grief.

> 14 *I have understood that whatever God does, it shall be for ever; nothing can be added to it, nor any thing taken from it because God does it that men should fear before him.*

This is the way God works. It's not the way man works.

Where does God desire to work?

He desires to effect a great change in our hearts and to transform our entire being. Then he will be able to work through us and touch others.

> 15 *That which has been is now, and that which is to be has already been and God shall seek that which is past.*

The Word of Life (from the beginning) is the Lord Jesus (John 1:1). Jesus has been and is now. He is to be and has already been. Jesus came as a man and returned to his former glory. Early references to him were veiled, so no one could discern them with their own understanding prior to his incarnation. God's plan of redemption was a mystery (even to brilliant intellectuals like Solomon) until the Holy Spirit was poured out upon the people of God. The seed of God's redemptive plan has existed since the beginning. The references are there and the prophecies existed, but it was a rare individual who understood them at the time. Certainly the Devil and his followers never understood God's plan.

> 16 *And moreover I saw under the sun that instead of judgment, there was wickedness; and instead of righteousness, that iniquity was there.*

> 17 *I said in my heart, God shall judge the righteous and the wicked; for there is a time determined to judge every will and regarding everything that is done.*

Everyone and everything will be judged. Each person will be responsible before God for everything that he has done.

The Devil has tried to position himself above the realm of what will be judged, but the Lord will judge him. In fact, he is presently being judged by the consequences of his actions. The crime that he committed regarding Eve has been added to the crime that he committed against the Lord Jesus in trying to have him killed on earth, along with everything else that he has done against the people of God.

> 18 *I said in my heart concerning the estate of*
> *the sons of men that God might manifest them*
> *and that they might see that they themselves*
> *are beasts one to another.*

When the revelation of God shines forth and his light penetrates our soul, when we have a direct encounter with the Lord and can see ourselves in his light, then all the lies of the enemy come tumbling down. This is what happened to the apostle Paul. He had thought that he was serving God, until Jesus appeared to him on the road to Damascus and he fell to the ground before the blinding light of the Lord (Acts 9:1-9). This light was so intense that his natural eyes were blinded, but soon he was able to see by the Spirit that he had really been acting like a beast. Then he could see that all the things he had been doing that he thought were right were atrocious in God's eyes.

> 19 *For that which befalls the sons of men*
> *befalls beasts; even one thing befalls them:*
> *as the one dies, so dies the other; and they all*
> *have one breath; so that a man has no more*
> *breath than a beast: for all is vanity.*

The biological life that we have is of the same quality as that of the beasts. Our physical lives have a beginning and an end, just as theirs do. If man has a dead soul and is not in contact with the Spirit of God, he is really nothing more than a beast. If you don't believe me, just read the newspapers. The headlines report one beastly deed after another. Deplorable though this may be, it is normal for the natural man.

> 20 *All go unto one place; all are of the dust and all shall turn to dust again.*
>
> 21 *Who knows that the spirit of the sons of men goes upward and that the spirit of the beast goes downward to the earth?*

Who knows?

Solomon didn't know.

At the time of Solomon, only two cases had been documented in Scripture where the spirit of man went upward, not downward like a beast's. I'm referring to Enoch and Moses, and even the case of Moses isn't clear in the Old Testament without support from the gospels and the book of Jude.

Enoch walked with God and did not see death (Hades) because God took him, yet he is included in Paul's list of heroes who *died in faith* (Hebrews 11:13). The fact that Enoch did not see death means that he went directly into the presence of God and wasn't detained in Hades like the other patriarchs, including Abraham.

Moses died obeying God when he was told to go up into the mountain and die. Jude 9 describes a fight over the body of Moses, and we know that the archangel Michael won this dispute with the Devil because Moses was present on the Mount of Transfiguration prior to the redemptive death and resurrection of Jesus Christ. Later, there was also the case of Elijah.[2]

> 22 *Therefore I perceive that there is nothing better than that a man should rejoice in his own works; for that is his portion; for who shall bring him to see what shall be after him?*

Solomon, with all his wisdom under the sun, didn't have the answer to this. He did not have the revelation that is available to us now.

The only one who can give us this revelation is the Lord Jesus by the Spirit of God. In the time of Solomon, the Spirit of God was only upon a person here or there, not upon all of the people of God. Normally, the anointing was only upon prophets, priests, or kings, all of whom had prepared their hearts to follow the Lord, one at a time.

Now, after the work of redemption of our Lord Jesus Christ, the Spirit of God can be upon anyone who prepares their heart to follow God.

How can we prepare our hearts to follow the Lord?

We must be willing to receive the correction of our heavenly Father. Those who do not receive correction cannot learn. If we can learn from the mistakes of others, we need not repeat them.

Solomon had to learn the hard way, after doing many things that the Lord had forbidden, including marrying hundreds of pagan women who contaminated the spiritual atmosphere in Israel with demonic, bloodthirsty idols.

2 Russell Stendal, *Elijah and Elisha* (Abbotsford, Wis.: ANEKO Press).

Let us pray

Lord,

We ask that you may deliver us and continue to deliver us from any tendency to trust in ourselves. We ask that by your Spirit you may complete the good work that you have begun in us. We ask that you will cleanse us and continue to keep us clean so we may participate in your work and desist from our own. We ask that we may invest our time and resources according to your will so we will reap eternal rewards, instead of investing in temporal things that will soon be lost. Amen.

Chapter Four

Is there Comfort for the Oppressed?

1 *So I returned and considered all the violence that is done under the sun and behold the tears of such as are oppressed, and they have no comforter; and on the side of their oppressors there was power; but the oppressed had no comforter.*

2 *Therefore I praised the dead who are already dead more than the living who are yet alive.*

3 *And I thought that better is he than both of them who has not been, who has not seen the evil works that are done under the sun.*

Note that the preaching of Solomon seems to have a different slant than almost all of the rest of the Bible. Today this type of message might be labeled left wing, even extreme left wing. However, as my friend Celso Macias is fond of pointing out, all of us have our hearts on the left side of our body.

Those on the left are very upset with the injustice that they see all around us. They are concerned for those who are oppressed. Yet many times, the politics and the projects that they put together to help the oppressed don't solve the problem. Sometimes the remedy they implement is worse than the disease.

Solomon contemplated all of these things: the violence that is done under the sun, the tears of the oppressed, and the fact that they have no comforter.

The Lord Jesus preached a message that's a bit different from Solomon's but uses similar terminology. He said, *Blessed are those who mourn for they shall be comforted* (Matthew 5:4).

Solomon said that there is no comforter. Jesus said that there is one. Jesus told his disciples that after his death, the Father would send the Comforter (John 14:26). The Comforter is the Holy Spirit, made available by the redemptive work of the Lord Jesus (John 16:7).

At the time of Solomon, the oppressed had no comforter.

Who are the oppressed today?

Just about everyone in the world today seems to be oppressed in one way or another.

> 1b *on the side of their oppressors there was power; but the oppressed had no comforter.*

Who are the oppressors?

The power in the world is currently in the hands of Satan, known as the prince of this world (John 12:31; 14:30; 16:11). Satan holds and consolidates his power through worship of "the beast." As we saw in the previous chapter, this is another name for the natural man without God. Satan deceives fallen humanity into worshipping man instead of God. Scripture states that in the world it is impossible to buy or sell without the mark of the beast in the person's hand or in their forehead (Revelation 13:16-17). This mark is primarily a way of acting and thinking according to the natural man under the sun – without God. Therefore, all those with the mark of the beast are busy oppressing one another, even in the midst of their humanistic worship of man.

Solomon said:

> 2 *Therefore I praised the dead who are already dead more than the living who are yet alive.*
>
> 3 *And I thought that better is he than both of them who has not been, who has not seen the evil works that are done under the sun.*

Things were so bad from Solomon's viewpoint that life wasn't worth living. He was not optimistic. With everything that he had, everything that he did, and everything that he knew, he was in turmoil as he came to the conclusion that none of this had truly satisfied him.

Solomon had much in common with those on the extreme left today who desire to correct social injustice as they perceive violence and oppression all around. They see the tears of the oppressed but don't seem able to solve the problem. When they are in power, sometimes they seem to do more harm than good, especially to those whom they purport to be rescuing from oppression.

> 4 *Again, I considered all travail and every right work, that for this a man is envied of his neighbor. This is also vanity and vexation of spirit.*

Sometimes we receive opposition and acquire enemies from places where we never imagined they would appear. If we go to a poor neighborhood and help a poor and oppressed family until they are on their feet, do you know what will inevitably happen?

The neighbors will soon become consumed with envy of that family and resentment against us for only helping that particular family. Solomon was aware of this, and therefore he said:

> 5 *The fool folds his hands together and eats his own flesh.*

The fool becomes so eaten up with envy that he consumes himself.

When the Lord helps us or sends someone to help us solve our problems, this is not the time to cross our hands and do nothing, nor is it the time to store up surplus things for ourselves. When the Lord straightens our path and blesses us, he wants to see if we will reach out and give others a hand up. This is the only way to overcome the envy that will surround us if God begins to really bless us materially.

We are to overcome evil with good (Romans 12:21). We will find, however, that we must do this with much more intensity than we would at first imagine. If we are to overcome, we must put our hearts and souls into planting that which is good.

We can only do this if the Lord has cleansed our hearts and if we are not seeking personal or even corporate gain.

> 6 *Better is a handful with rest than both the hands full with travail and vexation of spirit.*

The Lord wants us to be satisfied with getting what we need. When we begin to hoard more than we need, we will find *travail and vexation of spirit.*

> 7 *Then I returned, and I saw another vanity under the sun.*
>
> 8 *It is the man who is alone, without a successor, who has neither son nor brother; yet is there no end of all his labour; neither is his eye satisfied with riches; neither saith he, For whom do I labour and bereave my soul of good? This is also vanity and sore travail.*

How many people are like this?

They are busy working night and day, obtaining the riches of this world. They have no idea whom they are going to leave it to, even if they have children or siblings. They compulsively pile up more and more wealth and have absolutely no desire to share any of it with anyone.

Those on the extreme left tend to blame people like this for all the trouble in the world. They call them the ruling class, and they think that class warfare is the solution.

In Scripture, however, there are only two classes of people, and neither one has to do with economics. There are those who have sought the truth and have allowed God to deal with them until their hearts have been changed, and there are those who have not. (In the highest sense, Jesus is the truth, even though many who are drawn to the truth may not initially recognize his name.)

The person who works hard and stores up great gain (without knowing to whom they will leave it) believes that they are doing very well. They take great pride in their work ethic and think that those who are not like them are lazy.

Yet when this goes to either extreme (and the natural man is inherently given over to extremes), monopolies (state or private) will form, and opportunities, particularly to those who are small and weak, will be denied. Then the cycle repeats itself on a much larger scale with those who have locked up the opportunities by hoarding more and more, and everyone else being eaten up with envy.

> 9 *Two are better than one because they have a better reward for their labour.*
>
> 10 *For if they fall, the one will lift up his fellow; but woe to him that is alone when he falls, for he has not another to help him up.*
>
> 11 *Again, if two sleep together, then they have heat, but how can one be warm alone?*
>
> 12 *And if one prevails against him, two shall withstand him; and a threefold cord is not quickly broken.*

Solomon, under the inspiration of the Holy Spirit (for all Scripture is inspired by God, as 2 Timothy 3:16 confirms), recognizes that whatever we are doing, it is not good to be alone. This is what God has said from the beginning (Genesis 2:18).

Sadly, there are many who walk alone. The rich, the so-called ruling class, are very prone to this. They do not share their secrets with anyone, and when they fall, they fall alone.

I also know of revolutionaries so dedicated to their cause that they grow incapable of intimate friendship with others. They become unwilling or unable to trust anyone.

This can even happen to the leaders of large churches or ministries that become program and performance orientated. They dedicate themselves to projects instead of focusing on people.

Can two walk together unless they are in agreement (Amos 3:3)? What about three?

God's plan is to deal with us one by one and bring us under his authority and correction. Then, when our hearts are clean, he can join us to everyone else who has a clean heart. Man gets this backwards, however. Leaders attempt to form a large group or movement first and then wonder why they are having so much trouble fighting internal division among their mixed multitude of followers (Exodus 12:38; Nehemiah 13:3).

Jesus said that if two or three are gathered together in his name, he will be in their midst (Matthew 18:20). We may ask what we will in his name from his Father in heaven (John 14:13-14). This, of course, means that we must first be in agreement with Jesus.

The solution to these social problems will never be found in all the varying doctrines of right or left wing politics. Even those who pride themselves in seeking and representing what they see as the pragmatic center will fail. As long as the people feel oppressed and hurt, and most participate in the oppression of others, there will never be unity. And unity is sorely needed, because every house divided against itself will eventually fall (Matthew 12:25).

> 13 *Better is a poor and a wise child than an old and foolish king who will no longer be admonished.*

Jesus said we must become like a little child to enter the kingdom of heaven (Matthew 18:3).

Many of us would prefer to be a king, but all of us are like kings, because we have each been given a sovereign will by our Creator. Even God will not force himself upon us. If we consider our own reasoning to be absolutely right and the center of our focus is upon ourselves, we will feel oppressed by others even as we continue to unconsciously (or consciously) oppress those who disagree with us.

> 14 *For he came out of prison to reign, even though he was born poor into his kingdom.*

In the highest sense, the one who fits this description is Jesus Christ. He was born poor into his kingdom. All of us were born here, under the sun, into a fallen world of bondage, yet Jesus chose to come and join us in our oppressed state caused by the world, the flesh, and the Devil. He gave his life to redeem us, and when he died, he descended into Hades, the prison run by the Devil, who had trapped the souls of virtually everyone by death. But Jesus led captivity captive and took the keys of Hades and of death from Satan. He came out of prison to reign, and he is now seated at the right hand of the Father with all authority (Luke 22:69; 1 Peter 3:22).

> 15 *I saw all the living who are under the sun walking with the child, the successor that shall stand up in his stead.*

Jesus came so we might have life, so we can be born again into the nature of God instead of being spiritually dead like beasts. At the time of Jesus' birth, Herod, an old and foolish king, attempted to kill him, but in vain. Jesus is the beginning (the first of the first fruits) of the new creation that will replace the race of foolish old kings descended from Adam. All those whose souls are spiritually alive will walk with the child.

> 16 *There is no end of all the people that have been before them; those also that come after shall not be content in him. Surely this also is vanity and vexation of spirit.*

No one will ever be content, fulfilled, or satisfied in the old fallen human nature that all of us inherited from our ancestor, Adam. Everything having to do with the old man is vanity and vexation of spirit. Those who, like the religious hypocrites of Jesus' day, self-righteously cling to the old nature will never be content in it. Indeed, Jesus is a threat to their entire order of life. This is why they killed him.

From the time of Solomon, a thousand years would pass before the first coming of the Lord Jesus as a baby in Bethlehem. It took the victorious life, death, and resurrection of Jesus for us to be able to have the indwelling presence of the Comforter so we will not have to walk alone. Because of that victory over death, we can now walk with Jesus and with God the Father 24/7. And we have a bond by the Spirit with everyone who has a clean heart (or fervently desires to have one) and is walking with them too.

According to Scripture, three thousand years passed from Adam to the kingdom of Solomon. From Solomon to us, another three thousand years passed. We are now on the eve of the second coming of Jesus Christ, when the kingdom of God will visibly dominate the earth.

Let us pray

Lord,
We thank you for placing us in this present unique time in history. We have great expectations regarding your imminent return. May we be found clean and upright, in the center of your will, at your return. Amen.

Chapter Five

The Sacrifice of Fools

In Bible times, Israel had two calendars: the agricultural and the sacred. Neither one of them coincides with our modern calendar. Their agricultural calendar began near the end of February or early March and their sacred calendar had its New Year on the Feast of Trumpets, the first day of the seventh month of the agricultural calendar (near our first of October). Both calendars are lunar based.

> 1 *Watch thy feet when thou goest to the house of God and draw near with more willingness to hear than to give the sacrifice of fools, for they do not know how to do what God wants.*

Some go to the house of God as foolish hypocrites to speak, while others go in humility and repentance. Under the law, the Israelites were only required to attend the annual feasts described in Leviticus 23. In general terms, this consisted of the Passover (the fourteenth day of the first month), Pentecost (the day after the seventh Sabbath after Passover – always a Sunday), and Tabernacles (starting the fifteenth day of the seventh month and lasting for one week). Synagogues and weekly meetings are not mandated anywhere in Scripture.

In spiritual terms, Jesus is our Passover Lamb. He is the Lamb of God who takes away the sins of the world (John 1:29). His sacrifice has redeemed us once and for all and has given us the opportunity to be born again by the Spirit of God. Pentecost symbolizes the infilling of the Holy Spirit that is essential for the regeneration of lost and fallen humanity (Acts 2). Tabernacles, the feast of the fullness of the harvest, symbolizes God's plan to dwell (tabernacle) with his people for all eternity (Hosea 6:2, Revelation 21:3). The prophetic fullness of Tabernacles comes at the end of the church age, which is upon us.

Jesus told the Samaritan woman that the time would come, and now is, when the true worshippers would not worship in any specific place but in spirit and in truth (John 4:23). The New Testament is clear that those who are led by the Spirit are not under the law and that now, as the people of God, *we* are the temple (Galatians 5:18; 1 Corinthians 3:16). The law points out sin but does not have the ability to make us clean. Only by the Spirit are we able to put to death the deeds of the flesh and live (Romans 8:13).

We should obey if the Spirit of God leads us to a given place or meeting. But if we are attending out of religious obligation to relieve feelings of guilt, to impress God, or for any other human reason, then our attendance to religious rites and rituals could be a mistake. The Holy

Spirit will lead and guide each individual and show them how to invest their time and resources in a manner that is pleasing to God and will reap eternal reward.

> 2 *Do not be rash with thy mouth and do not let thy heart be hasty to utter any thing before God, for God is in heaven and thou upon the earth; therefore let thy words be few.*

If you visit religious places, you will notice that instead of few words, the prevailing tendency is quite the opposite. We are to let *our* words be few. (However, when God chooses to speak through someone, this is quite another matter.)

> 3 *For out of the preoccupation comes the dream, and the voice of the fool out of a multitude of words.*

The fears or preoccupations of religious people cause them to dream up rules and ritual in the midst of many words. From the perspective of God, people and the words they speak are either clean or unclean. People are either wise or they are fools. If we have the life of Jesus and the Holy Spirit links us to him and to the Father, we are among the wise.

Apart from God there is no real wisdom. We can't truly please God by fulfilling religious rituals and implementing what we think are godly principles according to our own human understanding (or according to the human understanding of those who would have us be under their spiritual covering and control).

> 4 *When thou dost vow a vow unto God, do*

not defer to pay it; for he has no pleasure in fools; pay that which thou hast vowed.

5 *It is better than thou should not vow than that thou should vow and not pay.*

Solomon wrote this a thousand years before the advent of Jesus Christ, who made the following statement: *Again, ye have heard that it was said to the ancients, Thou shalt not perjure thyself, but shalt perform unto the Lord thine oaths; but I say unto you, Swear not at all; neither by the heaven, for it is God's throne, nor by the earth, for it is his footstool, neither by Jerusalem, for it is the city of the great King. Neither shalt thou swear by thy head because thou canst not make one hair white or black. But let your communication be, Yes, yes; No, no; for whatsoever is more than that comes of evil* (Matthew 5:33-37).

Religion, influenced and controlled by man, attempts to indoctrinate the people and obligate them to swear unwavering faith in their dogmas and creeds. The leaders encourage people to vow to go to all their meetings, pay them their tithes, and submit to their spiritual direction. Repetition of prayers, songs of worship, offerings, and endless religious ritual may soon take the place of a spontaneous relationship with God from the heart.

6 *Suffer not thy mouth to cause thy flesh to sin; neither say thou before the angel, that it was ignorance. Why should thou cause God to be angry because of thy voice and destroy the work of thine hands?*

Many religious people suffer under great mountains of

guilt because someone squeezed them into promising things that may have seemed right at the time but were not the perfect will of God. Only when we hear the voice of God for ourselves (and if we embrace what he says with faith), can abundant grace be available to us by the Holy Spirit to do his will.

The Jews spent fifteen hundred years trying to keep God's commandments in their own strength, even as their religious leaders kept adding endless dogmas, rites, procedures, meetings, and rituals invented by themselves. The people failed hopelessly at complying with this plethora of rules and regulations.

Jesus perfectly fulfilled the law, but the Scripture states that *he would not walk in Jewry because the Jews sought to kill him* (John 7:1 KJV). They had so changed and twisted the word of God that most of them could not even recognize the living Word when he walked among them.

Eventually God became so angry regarding the extraneous words that had been spoken in his name and the excessive demands that the leaders had imposed that the work of their hands was destroyed. Jerusalem and the temple were demolished on at least two occasions.

> *7 Because dreams abound, and vanities and*
> *the words are many, but fear thou God.*

The Jews felt very self-righteous as they attempted to fulfill all the religious rules and regulations they had dreamed up. This turned out to be vanity, however, for it is the fear of the Lord that is the beginning of wisdom (Psalm 111:10).

To fear the Lord is to have a profound respect for

him and live to please him in all that we say or do. God is deeply offended when people with unclean hands and unclean hearts, spewing forth a smoke screen of pious verbiage, attempt to represent him in a manner that he has not ordained.

> 8 *If thou seest violence unto the poor and the extortion of rights and justice in a province, do not marvel at the matter, for height is looking at height; and there is one higher than they.*

Man may think that he is autonomous, but our autonomy is limited. Only two kingdoms matter: one is of darkness and the other of light. A province dominated by violence against the poor and the extortion of rights and justice is in darkness.

Our fight is not against flesh and blood. It is *against principalities, against powers, against the lords of this age, rulers of this darkness, against spiritual wickedness in the heavens* (Ephesians 6:12). Yet there is one higher than they. Only as we listen to God and only as his Spirit moves us can we be clean and walk in victory. We cannot serve God and the lords of this age at the same time.

> 9 *And there is higher authority in all of the things of the earth, but he who serves the field is king.*

God plants his good seed in the field. In fact, according to Jesus, *we* are the good seed (Matthew 13:38). The kingdoms of man upon the earth are filled with those who seek personal gain and struggle to lord it over others.

But Jesus said that in his kingdom, the humble servant is the greatest (Mark 9:35).

> 10 *He that loves money shall not be satisfied with money; nor he that loves abundance with increase; this is also vanity.*
>
> 11 *When goods increase, those that eat them are increased; and what good is there to the owners thereof, except the beholding of them with their eyes?*
>
> 12 *The sleep of the servant is sweet whether he eats little or much, but the abundance of the rich will not suffer him to sleep.*

The servant works, gets tired, and has a good night's sleep. The more the rich person has, on the other hand, the less he is able to sleep because he is always trying to get more and not lose what he already has.

Notice where this goes:

> 13 *There is another sore evil which I have seen under the sun, namely riches kept for the owners thereof to their hurt;*
>
> 14 *which are lost by evil pursuits and to the sons which he has begotten: there is nothing left in his hand.*

I wonder how much rest the Devil gets. Since his kingdom doesn't run on love and trust, he must expend much effort keeping his "sons" in line, for the threat that some of his followers will attempt to depose him always exists.

Ill-gotten gains come with a curse, not a blessing. This applies to every evil person.

> 15 *As he came forth of his mother's womb, naked shall he return to go as he came and shall take nothing of his labour, which he may carry away in his hand.*

Unless earthly riches are invested in things of eternal value, there will be absolutely nothing to show for them in the end.

Ministers who manipulate their congregation by using feelings of guilt will never be able to invest in the eternal. All that is not inspired and empowered by the Spirit of God will be eternally sterile and void. This also relates to the sacrifice of fools mentioned in the first verse of this chapter. Those who solicit or give the sacrifice of fools will never know how to do what God wants.

> 16 *And this also is a sore evil; that in all points as he came, so shall he go: and what profit has he that has laboured for the wind?*

> 17 *In addition to this, all the days of his life he shall eat in darkness, with much wrath and pain and sorrow sickness.*

We know that Satan and his followers demonstrate much wrath and frustration. Satan knows (or will soon know) that his time is now very short (Revelation 12:12). When it finally dawns on his followers that they have *labored for the wind*, they will be overcome with pain and *sorrow sickness.* Scripture describes the time when they will realize that they are in total darkness and gnaw their tongues for pain (Revelation 16:10). They will all come down with sorrow sickness.

What will be the future of those who do not have a healthy relationship with God the Father?

Think about it!

> 18 *Behold therefore the good which I have seen: that good is to eat and to drink and to enjoy of the good of all his labour that he takes under the sun all the days of his life, which God gives him, for it is his portion.*
>
> 19 *Likewise, unto every man to whom God has given riches and wealth, he has also given him power to eat thereof and to take his portion and to rejoice in his labour; this is the gift of God.*
>
> 20 *To such a one, God will remove the concerns common to others, for God shall answer him with joy from his heart.*

Things that are good and are approved by God are much different from ill-gotten gains. We are allowed to freely enjoy and partake of all that is good. In the highest sense, the Lord Jesus Christ is the gift of God, and believing and trusting in him as our only Lord and Savior is the only way that we can come back into a right relationship with God the Father (John 3:16). When we receive good things from God and labor together with him, we are also given the right to eat and drink and enjoy the good of all of our labor here in this world under the sun. In fact, God will even remove the *concerns common to others* as we receive the answer directly from him. Joy is the fruit of the Holy Spirit (Galatians 5:22). When we begin to feel joy from the heart of God and know in our heart that he is pleased with us, we find true satisfaction.

Jesus said:

> *No one can serve two masters, for either he will hate the one and love the other or else he will hold to the one and despise the other. Ye cannot serve God and riches. Therefore I say unto you, Take no thought for your life, what ye eat or what ye shall drink, nor yet for your body, what ye shall put on. Is not the life more than food, and the body than raiment?*
>
> *Behold the fowls of the air, for they sow not, neither do they reap nor gather into barns, yet your heavenly Father feeds them. Are ye not much better than they?*
>
> *Which of you by taking thought can add one cubit unto his stature? And why take ye thought for raiment? Consider the lilies of the field, how they grow: they toil not, neither do they spin; and yet I say unto you, That even Solomon in all his glory was not arrayed like one of these. Therefore, if God so clothes the grass of the field, which today is and tomorrow is cast into the oven, shall he not much more clothe you, O ye of little faith?*

> *Therefore take no thought, saying, What shall we eat? or, What shall we drink? or, With what shall we be clothed? (For the Gentiles seek after all these things.) For your heavenly Father knows that ye have need of all these things. But seek ye first the kingdom of God and his righteousness, and all these things shall be added unto you.*
>
> *Take therefore no thought for the morrow, for the morrow shall take thought for the things of itself. Sufficient unto the day is the affliction thereof* (Matthew 6:24-34).

Jesus' words also have spiritual application. If we feed on what he says (for he is the Bread of Life) and drink from the living water flowing from his life and allow him to cover us by the Holy Spirit, then we don't have to worry about tomorrow.

When God gives us natural or spiritual things and we share our blessings with those whom God puts upon our hearts, joy flows into us from the heart of God. This will cause us to rise above all the toil and affliction that we find here, under the sun.

Solomon himself finally understood that true joy flows only from the heart of God.

Let us pray

> *Heavenly Father,*
> *We ask for all those who are still mulling over the issues of life, for those who are beginning*

to see that everything they invested in is really vanity and vexation of spirit, for those who feel trapped and oppressed – May they, like Solomon, discover the joy that flows from your heart alone. We ask this in the name of our Lord Jesus Christ. Amen.

Chapter Six

The Woman More Bitter than Death

1 *There is another evil which I have seen under the sun, and it is very common among men:*

2 *A man to whom God has given riches, wealth, and honour so that he lacks nothing for his soul of all that he desires, yet God does not give him power to eat of it, but the strangers eat it; this is vanity, and it is an evil disease.*

The previous chapter mentions the sacrifice of fools and the kinds of riches that are detrimental to their owners. Now Solomon alludes to those who have God-given riches, wealth, and honor, but are unable to enjoy any of them.

Notice that this evil also occurs *under the sun*. This is what happens in the world. If we are of the world, it may prove to be impossible to enjoy God-given blessings. Lot and his family experienced this when they chose to live in Sodom. It happened to many Jews of Jesus' day when they were unable to enjoy his words and miracles and be nourished and edified by them. In the end, God sent the gospel to the Gentiles, and Jerusalem, like Sodom, soon came to nothing (it became mere vanity).

> 3 *If a man begets a hundred sons and lives many years so that the days of his years are many, if his soul is not filled with good and also that he have no burial; I say that an aborted birth is better than he.*

How could a dead person have no burial? It literally happened to evil Queen Jezebel when she met her gruesome ending (2 Kings 9:33-37), and Scripture states that it will also happen to the Devil (Isaiah 14:20-21).

What is Solomon talking about?

In the light of the New Testament, we know that baptism symbolizes the burial of the old man (or old nature) and new birth into the life of Jesus Christ (Romans 6:3-5). If there has been no such burial, the old man has not been dealt with.

The reference to a hundred sons speaks of fulfilling the plan of God regarding evangelism, yet Paul said, *but I keep my body under, and bring it into subjection, lest preaching to others, I myself should become reprobate* (1 Corinthians 9:27).

Are spiritual births being aborted in the church today? Is the corrupt life of Adam being reproduced instead of the life of Christ?

> 4 *For he came in vain and departs unto darkness, and his name shall be covered with darkness.*
>
> 5 *Even though he has not seen the sun nor known anything; this one has more rest than the other.*
>
> 6 *For though the other should live a thousand years twice and has not enjoyed good; both shall surely go to the same place.*

Solomon built the temple according to the plan of God; he had so many women that he could have literally begotten more than a hundred sons, and he led and judged the people of Israel under the sun with wisdom that he received from God. In spite of all this, Solomon expressed deep concern that he had not been able to enjoy or feed upon the good things he had received from God. In the end, he thought that even an aborted child would have more rest than he did and they would both go to the same place!

> 6 *For though the other should live a thousand years twice and has not enjoyed good; both shall surely go to the same place.*

A thousand years twice (two thousand years) is a mention of the church age, an age in which much of the reign of Solomon is symbolic. After the day of Pentecost when the glory of God fell upon a new temple made of living stones, the church became increasingly devoted to her own works and an obsession with "women" (symbolic of different sects, congregations, and denominations) that got out of control, leading to widespread idolatry. For one reason or another, much of the church has been unable to enjoy the good things that God has made available. Solomon apparently repented and returned to the Lord before he died. What will happen with today's church?

> 7 *All the labour of man is for his mouth, and with all this the appetite is not filled.*

The work of the natural man will never ever be able to satisfy his carnal appetites.

Jesus said, *Blessed are those who hunger and thirst for righteousness, for they shall be satisfied* (Matthew 5:6).

Righteousness is being and doing what God desires and requires a spiritual new birth and the indwelling, regenerating presence of the Holy Spirit. This is where Solomon was hung up. He found it virtually impossible to enjoy the good things that God had given him. Nor was he alone in this. He was astute enough to perceive that under the sun, this condition is very common among men.

> 8 *For what has the wise more than the fool? what more has the poor that knows how to walk among the living?*

> 9 *It is better to enjoy the good that is present than the wandering of desire; this is also vanity and vexation of spirit.*

Jesus said, *Blessed are the poor in spirit, for theirs is the kingdom of the heavens* (Matthew 5:3). The poor in spirit are those who have allowed God to deal with their pride and arrogance. This is what the truly wise person has more than the fool – they have the wisdom to know how much they need God. And this is why the poor person knows how to walk among the living (among those who are born again in the life of Jesus Christ). No money is needed to be born again in Christ.

All of us experience *wandering desires* from time to time – desires that have the possibility of pulling us out of the way of the Lord. God wants us to enjoy the good that is present and stop thinking that the grass is greener on the other side of the fence. The *wandering of desire* will bring us back to vanity and vexation of spirit if we give in to the impulses of the flesh.

The most intensive spiritual warfare will be encountered after we are born again. When we were slaves to the world, the flesh, and the Devil, we were unable to do anything except sin. After we are set free, we have a clear choice. We may yield to God and, by the Spirit, put to death the deeds of the flesh, or we may return to the sin and bondage that leads to spiritual death (Romans 8:13).

> 10 *He that is has been named already; and it*
> *is known that he is man and that he shall not*
> *be able to contend with him that is mightier*
> *than he.*

If we don't understand this, we don't understand anything. The Devil is stronger than we are. The flesh is stronger than we are. The only way that we can dominate is by the grace of God in the new man in Christ.

> 11 *Certainly the many words multiply vanity,*
> *what more does man have?*

> 12 *For who knows what is good for man in*

> *this life, all the days of the life of his vanity which he causes to be as a shadow? for who shall teach the man what shall be after him under the sun?*

Under the sun, man thinks that he is progressing and will continue to evolve into a super creature. According to the reality of God, however, man is not progressing. Our corrupt human nature continues to degenerate. Man, who was created in the image of God, is turning back into an animal. If you don't believe me, read the newspapers or listen to the news. They describe one beastly event after another.

Ecclesiastes 7

> 1 *A good name is better than precious ointment and the day of death than the day of one's birth.*

Precious ointment or anointing oil is a symbol of gifts and ministries from God, who is no respecter of persons. God is willing to pour out his Spirit on all of humankind, hoping that by the Spirit we will put to death the deeds of the flesh.

The only way to have a good name is to become part of the family of God. His name (nature) is the only good one. The sons of God are those who are led by the Spirit of God (Romans 8:14). Those who use the *precious ointment* to obtain personal gain in their fallen natural state may eventually discover, possibly too late, that a good name is better than precious ointment (Matthew 7:22-23).

In the spiritual realm the day of the actual death of

the old man is even better than the day of our new birth in Christ. For flesh and blood cannot inherit the kingdom of God. Samson was an interesting and intriguing example of what may be called a good day of death (Judges 16:30). Samson called on the Lord for strength, and in his death he destroyed more of his enemies than he ever did during the rest of his life.

> 2 *It is better to go to the house of mourning than to go to the house of feasting, for that is the end of all men, and the living will lay it to his heart.*

Jesus said, *Blessed are those that mourn for they shall be comforted* (Matthew 5:4). Remember that the Holy Spirit is the Comforter.

If we place our lives upon the altar of God, anything that he does not like or approve of will go up in smoke. Those who use the blessings and gifts of God not to help others but to build themselves a *house of feasting* to bolster their pride, arrogance, and ego may miss their opportunity to have a right relationship with God.

> 3 *Sorrow is better than laughter; for by the sadness of the countenance the heart is made whole.*

If our heart is not made whole, it does not matter how many benefits we obtain, how many things we own, or how many gifts God has given us. It doesn't even matter what level of anointing or ministry we have attained. If our heart is not made whole, nothing else really matters.

> 4 *The heart of the wise is in the house of*

mourning, but the heart of fools is in the house of pleasure.

The Comforter, the Holy Spirit, is in the house of mourning. The fools who congregate in the house of pleasure, a house of nothing more than happy-clappy feelings, may receive a spirit that is supernatural but not holy. The congregation whoops it up and confuses the realm of the soul with the realm of the spirit. Soon the entire "house" is performance oriented until every residue of the real Holy Spirit is quenched.

5 *It is better to hear the rebuke of the wise than to hear the song of fools.*

When the Holy Spirit is grieved, we had best stop what we are doing and listen. God may choose to use someone who is wise to rebuke us. Otherwise, the song of fools will drown out the voice of the Spirit, which will not force itself upon our notice.

6 *The laughter of the fool is as the crackling of thorns under a pot, and this also (the laughter or prosperity of the fool) is vanity.*

Fools are prone to follow what they perceive as supernatural experiences instead of the still, small voice of the Lord. Anyone who takes their eyes off God to follow the fools flocking to the latest spiritual fad will soon be deceived. The sometimes hysterical laughter of the fool is like the crackling of the fire, burning up the thorns under the pot of all the perversion that the fools cook up.

7 *Surely oppression makes a wise man mad, and a gift destroys the heart.*

Oppression is closely linked to corruption. The injustice can drive a wise man insane, and a gift or bribe will destroy our hearts if we allow someone to buy us.

> 8 *Better is the end of a thing than its beginning, and he who has suffered in spirit is better than the proud in spirit.*

It may take suffering in spirit to defeat our pride so that we may become poor in spirit. Pride and arrogance are diametrically opposed to the kingdom of God.

> 9 *Do not be hasty in thy spirit to be angry, for anger rests in the bosom of fools.*

Scripture states that *the wrath of man does not work the righteousness of God* (James 1:20).

> 10 *Never say, What is the cause that the former days were better than these? for thou dost not enquire wisely concerning this.*

The world has been under a curse since the beginning of the rebellion against God, and the only way out from under this is in the life of Christ. We cannot look back on former good old days to solve our problems. Our hope is in the future return of our Lord Jesus Christ and the future fullness of the kingdom of God.

> 11 *Knowledge is good with an inheritance and is the excellency of those that see the sun.*

> 12 *For knowledge is a defense, and money is a defense; but wisdom excels in that it gives life to those that have it.*

The knowledge and inheritance available to those of

this world is the excellence of those who see the sun. Knowledge and money are a defense, but only wisdom can tell us how to properly use them to invest in heavenly things far beyond the sun. Only wisdom can show us the path to life.

The best knowledge is the knowledge of God, which is good and has an inheritance. The only inheritance that really matters is that we be joint heirs with Christ (Romans 8:16-17).

> 13 *Consider the work of God; for who can make straight that which he has twisted?*

God is the one who placed the earth under the curse, and only he can straighten it out again. The only way that we, as individuals, can be straightened out is if we participate in the life of Jesus Christ.

> 14 *In the day of good enjoy that which is good, but in the day of adversity open your eyes and learn: God also has made the one (the day of adversity) before the other, to the end that man should find nothing after him.*

> 15 *All things have I seen in the days of my vanity: there is a just man that perishes for his righteousness, and there is a wicked man that prolongs his days by his wickedness.*

Who is the just man that laid down his life for his righteousness?

He is Jesus and the many-membered body of Christ.

Jesus said, *He that loses his life for my sake shall find it* (Matthew 10:39).

Who is the wicked man that prolongs his days by his wickedness?

Satan and his followers are using every wicked trick they can think of to prolong their days yet will soon run out of time (Revelation 12:12).

> 16 *Do not be too legalistic; neither make thyself over wise in thine own eyes: why should thou destroy thyself?*

Satan has used legalism, self-righteous spiritual pride, and hypocrisy to destroy the Jews. He has also employed these same tactics to overcome large sectors of the church. *For the letter kills, but the Spirit gives life* (2 Corinthians 3:6).

> 17 *Do not be too hasty to condemn, neither be thou foolish: why should thou die in the midst of thy labours?*

Jesus said, *Judge not, that ye be not judged* (Matthew 7:1).

> 18 *It is good that thou should take hold of this; and also from the other not withdraw thy hand; for he that fears God shall come through with everything.*

We should not be judgmental, but at the same time we should not withdraw our hand from righteousness and justice. The fear of the Lord is the beginning of wisdom, which is the key to coming through with everything – to having *all these things … added unto you* (Matthew 6:33).

> 19 *Wisdom strengthens the wise more than ten mighty men who are in the city.*

In Solomon's day, you could say that the city of Jerusalem was founded on the Ten Commandments, which the children of Israel attempted to implement in their own natural strength. Wisdom will deliver us from the kind of legalism into which those human efforts degenerated. Jesus' interpretation of the law, contained in the Sermon on the Mount, has been called the constitution of the kingdom of God (Matthew 5-7).

> 20 *For surely there is not a just man upon earth that in doing good does not sin.*

At the time of Solomon, there had never been a just person who had not sinned in one way or another. The only one who has never sinned is our Lord Jesus Christ. Our only path to victory is in the life of Christ (Philippians 4:13). Only by the indwelling power of the Holy Spirit can regeneration may take place. Only by the Spirit can we put to death the deeds of the flesh and live (Romans 8:13).

Much of what mankind does, believing it to be good, is really sin in the eyes of God. The simplest definition of sin is that it is going against the word of the Lord. Solomon made his first error when he married Pharaoh's daughter. He thought that he was doing good by using marriage to make political alliances with potential enemies, but after having a thousand women, he was definitely having second thoughts.

> 21 *Also do not take to heart all the words that are spoken lest thou hear thy slave speak evil of thee.*

> 22 *For thine own heart knows that thou thyself likewise hast spoken evil of others many times.*

One of Solomon's own "slaves," Jeroboam, eventually split the kingdom, taking most of it away from Solomon's son, Rehoboam. When he heard the prophetic words that had been spoken regarding Jeroboam, Solomon attempted to kill him, so the prophecy would not come to pass (1 Kings 11:26-40). In this case, Solomon was unable to keep his own advice. Like many of us, he was better at giving advice than taking it.

> 23 *All this I have proved by wisdom: I said, I will be wise, but it was far from me.*

The truth was dawning on Solomon. Even with all the God-given wisdom (under the sun) that he used in governing Israel, he was still far from being wise.

> 24 *That which has been is far off and that which is exceeding deep, who can find it out?*

God had exceedingly deep plans that would be fulfilled a thousand years into the future. He would send the Messiah, Jesus Christ, and so make the earnest or down payment of the Holy Spirit available to all believers (2 Corinthians 1:22; 5:5; Ephesians 1:9-14). Two thousand years after that event, we are expecting to receive the fullness of our inheritance in Christ, that is, the fullness of the Spirit. Solomon did come to realize that certain things have such depth that they can only be received by direct revelation from God. That, after all, is how he wrote this sermon!

> 25 *I applied my heart to know and to search and to seek out wisdom and the reason of things, and to know the wickedness of folly and the madness of error;*
>
> 26 *and I find more bitter than death the woman whose heart is snares and nets, and her hands are bonds; whosoever pleases God shall escape from her, but the sinner shall be held prisoner in her.*

Because he did not depend on God, Solomon was trapped for a long time by the snares and nets and bonds of pagan women who enticed him to worship their demonic gods. He directly experienced the wickedness of folly and the madness of error. He learned, as all sinners do, that sin is a prison. He also realized, by the revelation of the Spirit of God, that an escape route from this prison was available, because *whosoever pleases God shall escape from her*. But first he had to learn that *without faith it is impossible to please God, for he that comes to God must believe that he is and that he is a rewarder of those that diligently seek him* (Hebrews 11:6).

Each of Solomon's pagan wives represented a pagan nation or people group somewhere that had made an alliance with him through marriage. In the spiritual realm, women can represent congregations or entire denominations that attempt to make their own alliances with those who do not depend upon God. There are groups that employ snares and nets to bond the people to themselves instead of directly to God, because they do not recognize that Jesus is the only mediator between man and God (1

Timothy 2:5). Whosoever pleases God shall escape from her, the errant congregation or denomination. But since it is impossible to please God without faith, the sinner who has no faith shall continue to be held prisoner in her.

The religious institutions of man cannot deal with habitual sin and guilt. They have no power to forgive the sin and wash the sinner clean. Instead, they have learned how to use the sinner's emotions to further their own kingdoms. Their parishioners are constantly under a burden of guilt that they attempt to absolve by participating in religious rites and rituals. The leaders make a point of not telling us that we may take our sin directly to our Lord Jesus Christ, who is our high priest. He will help us place everything upon the altar of God, so the fire of God can destroy the power that sin has wielded over us. After dealing with sin, Jesus desires to help us deal with guilt until the fire of God consumes that as well. When God forgives our sin, he remembers it no more. He removes our rebellions as far as the east is from the west (Psalm 103:12).

Any time we are convicted by the Holy Spirit and made aware of anything that is wrong in our life (related to sin or guilt or anything else), we have an Advocate with the Father. Jesus promises that *if we confess our sins, he is faithful and just to forgive us our sins* ***and to cleanse us from all unrighteousness*** (1 John 1:9, author's emphasis). By faith in him, we can live victoriously in unbroken clean communion with God the Father.

27 *Behold, this I have found, saith the*

preacher, weighing things one by one to find out the answer,

28 *which my soul yet seeks, but I find not: one man among a thousand I have found, but a woman among all those I have not found.*

We must understand that Solomon is not writing this message or sermon on his own; the Spirit of God is speaking through Solomon. God can work, and has worked, through imperfect people. If he only worked through those who are perfect, who among us would qualify?

In Scripture, individual men and women of faith are referred to as sons of God (regardless of gender), and entire congregations, nations, or denominations can be referred to as women. When Solomon wrote this, he literally had a thousand women in his household, but apparently he had not yet found a single one who was trustworthy (1 Kings 11:3). (*Song of Solomon* was undoubtedly written later.)

During both the age of law and the age of grace, it has been impossible to find a perfect "woman" – a perfect corporate expression of the people of God. Yet we know that Jesus will return for a bride without spot or wrinkle or any such flaw (Ephesians 5:26-27). I believe that one of the next events on the prophetic calendar of God is the pouring out of the fullness of the Spirit (of which there are many types and shadows throughout prophetic Scriptures), which will set the stage for the return of Jesus Christ.

29 *Behold, this only have I found: that God has made man upright, but they have sought out many perversions.*

God did not make man depraved. God made man upright and declared all of his creation to be very good (Genesis 1:31). It is man who has used his own free will to seek out perversions of God's gifts (Genesis 6:5). The preaching of Solomon here is quite a bit different from many of the sermons that are heard in churches today.

Solomon's message deals with many age-old questions and veiled prophecies regarding events of the church age and beyond. Prosperity is the greatest test that God's people will ever face. It is extremely important that we learn from Solomon's experience.

Let us pray

Heavenly Father,
We ask that we may be able to learn from the mistakes of Solomon. May we guard our hearts above all else. May we appreciate the work that you accomplish in us. Like David, we ask you to search our hearts and deal with anything that you do not approve of. We ask this in the name of our Lord Jesus Christ.
Amen.

Chapter Seven

For Every Will There is Time and Judgement

1 *Who is as the wise man? and who is as he who knows the interpretation of all things? The wisdom of this man shall make his face to shine, and the coarseness of his face shall be changed.*

The only man who is truly wise is Jesus Christ. He is the only one who knows the interpretation of all things. Regarding *the coarseness of his face*, Scripture states, *There is no outward appearance in him, nor beauty* (Isaiah 53:2). After Jesus' resurrection, however, John wrote that his countenance was *as the sun when it shines in its strength* (Revelation 1:16).

2 *I counsel thee to keep the king's commandment and the word of the covenant that thou hast made with God.*

The true king of the people of God is the Lord Jesus Christ. His commandment is that we love one another (John 13:34). Our covenant is to love the Lord our God with all our heart, with all our soul, with all our mind, and with all our strength, and to love our neighbor as we love ourselves (Matthew 22:37-39; Mark 12:30-31).

> 3 *Do not be hasty to rebel against him; do not persist in any evil thing, for he shall do whatever pleases him;*

Despite these wise words, Solomon did enter into serious rebellion against God. Yet it appears that in the end, he decided not to persist in any evil thing. Therefore, although Solomon's sins are recorded in the book of Kings (likely accumulated by scribes), they are absent from the book of Chronicles (likely written by prophets or by priests at the temple), because when God forgives, he remembers our trespasses no more. Many tragic consequences of our wrong actions, however, go on into the future even after we are forgiven.

> 4 *because the word of the king is his power*
> *and who may say unto him, What doest thou?*

There may have been a time when Solomon felt with pride that the above verses applied to him, yet here is the word that the Lord spoke unto Solomon: *And the LORD became angry with Solomon because his heart was turned aside from the LORD God of Israel, who had appeared unto him twice, and had commanded him concerning this thing, that he should not go after other gods; but he did not keep that which the LORD commanded him.*

Therefore the LORD said unto Solomon, Because this has been in thee, and thou hast not kept my covenant and my statutes, which I commanded thee, I will surely rend the kingdom from thee and will give it to thy slave. But I will not do it in thy days for David, thy father's sake, but I will rend it out of the hand of thy son. However, I will not rend away all the kingdom, but will give one tribe to thy son for David, my slave's sake, and for Jerusalem's sake which I have chosen (1 Kings 11:9-13).

When he received this judgment from God, Solomon apparently decided to desist from the evil that he was involved in. The damage to his descendants, however, was very great.

> 5 *Whosoever keeps the commandment shall experience no evil thing, and a wise man's heart discerns both time and judgment.*

Solomon received a great spiritual heritage from his father, David. Unfortunately, despite all his reputed wisdom, he was unable to pass down a similar heritage to his own children because he repeatedly failed to keep his covenant with God (1 Kings 11). The pagan high places that he and his wives erected all over Israel remained a stumbling block to God's people for well over four hundred years.

> 6 *Because for every will there is time and judgment, because the evil of man is great upon him,*
>
> 7 *for he does not know that which shall be; nor when it shall be. Who will teach it to him?*

In his fallen state, even with gifts and blessings from

God (such as the wisdom that God gave to Solomon), the natural man will never know *that which shall be, nor when it shall be.* This revelation is only given to the born-again sons of God by the Spirit of God as they come to maturity in Christ.

> 8 *There is no man that has power over the spirit to retain the spirit; neither does he have power over the day of death, and weapons are of no use in that war; neither shall wickedness deliver those that are given to it.*

The first time that power over death is recorded in Scripture occurred many years later, when Elijah raised a boy from the dead. Something similar happened in the double portion ministry of Elisha. And even after Elisha's death, when a band of Moabite attackers was spied while someone was being buried, *they cast the man into the sepulchre of Elisha; and when the dead man touched the bones of Elisha, he revived, and stood up on his feet* (2 Kings 13:21).

All of this prefigures in type and shadow that Jesus Christ would overcome death and have power over it in resurrection. Jesus introduced very different spiritual weapons, starting with the truth, that are extremely effective in this war when natural weapons are useless (1 Corinthians 2:4-6).

Solomon also learned the hard way that worship of pagan gods (witchcraft and the occult) cannot deliver those who are given over to it.

> 9 *All this I have seen and applied my heart unto every work that is done under the sun:*

the time in which one man rules over another to his own hurt.

Here, Solomon is beginning to realize that ruthless kings hurt themselves as well as their subjects in the realm of this present world under the sun. Without the indwelling presence of the Spirit of God, we are all ruthless kings.

10 *Then I also saw that the wicked who were buried come into remembrance more than those who had frequented the holy place, and these were forgotten in the city where they worked uprightly. This also is vanity.*

And so it is even today. The wicked who are buried are more newsworthy than the godly priests who frequented the Holy Place. Now we are in the era of the priesthood of all believers, and those who work uprightly are mostly forgotten by the world around them after they pass away. God, however, keeps an accurate record of everything.

11 *Because the sentence against an evil work is not executed speedily, therefore the heart of the sons of men is fully set in them to do evil.*

Solomon was lucky that the sentence against his evil works was not executed speedily. God is very slow to anger, yet he did become angry against Solomon (1 Kings 11:9). The sentence was that God would rend the kingdom during the time of Solomon's son, not while Solomon was still alive to see it.

There are sons of men and there are sons of God. We begin our life on earth as the former, but the Lord desires for us to become the latter (Galatians 4:4-5).

> 12 *Though a sinner does evil one hundred times and his judgment is prolonged, yet surely I know that it shall be well with those that fear God, who fear before his presence;*
>
> 13 *but it shall never be well with the wicked, neither shall his days be prolonged, which are as a shadow, because he did not fear before the presence of God.*

Even though Solomon experienced virtually all that wickedness had to offer, in the end he repented in the fear of God. With his hundreds of pagan wives who enticed him into worshiping many pagan deities, Solomon must have done evil well over a hundred times (1 Kings 11:1-8). He came out of this convinced that although things shall never be well with the wicked, they shall be well with those who fear God. Solomon's book of Ecclesiastes even went down in history as Scripture inspired by the Holy Spirit (2 Timothy 3:16).

> 14 *There is another vanity which is done upon the earth: that there are just men, who are recompensed as if they had done according to the work of the wicked; again, there are wicked men, who are recompensed as if they had done according to the work of the righteous; I say that this also is vanity.*

Jesus, the first just man in human history, was crucified as if he had done the work of the wicked. Many of Jesus' followers have also been unjustly martyred for their faith. The repentant thief being crucified beside Christ, however, was told that he would be with him in Paradise.

Toward the end of his life, Solomon must have felt more and more like a wicked man who had been recompensed as if he had done according to the work of the righteous. His life's work culminated in what history calls the golden age of Israel; yet deep inside, Solomon knew that it was really vanity and vexation of spirit. Many of the great works of the church seem to be in the same category.

> 15 *Therefore I commended joy because a man has no better thing under the sun than to eat and to drink and to be merry, for that shall abide with him of his labour the days of his life, which God gives him under the sun.*

Real joy is the fruit of the Spirit and does not come at the command of the likes of Solomon; yet the kings of the people of God continue to command joy. They continue to preach that man has nothing better to do under the sun than to eat and drink and be merry at their contaminated rituals, festivals, pot lucks, conventions, and amusement events.

> 16 *Therefore I applied mine heart to know wisdom and to see the business that is done upon the earth (for also there is he that neither day nor night sees sleep with his eyes).*

God is watching us all the time.

> 17 *And I have seen regarding all the works of God that man cannot attain to understand the work that is being done under the sun,*

> *because though a man labours to seek it out, yet he shall not find it; even though the wise man says that he knows it, yet he shall not be able to attain it.*

What are the works of God?

If heaven and earth shall pass away, what are the works of God being done under the sun that shall remain? The natural man cannot perceive or understand the work that God is doing in the hearts of people like us. God can change corrupt, unclean sinners. He can make us part of his new creation where everything is based on justice and righteousness. Those who have the Spirit of God are able to understand and even participate in this work that the Lord is doing. Jesus Christ commands joy for those whom he has redeemed.

Throughout much of his reign, Solomon thought that it was important to construct buildings and cities, to make strategic alliances, and to acquire riches, horses, chariots, and women. In worldly terms, he was right, but in spiritual terms, Solomon was completely wrong.

He finally realized that everything that he had been doing was vanity and vexation of spirit. All of his famous *wisdom under the sun* could not compare to the true wisdom of God.

Let us pray

> *Lord,*
> *We thank you for the opportunity we have been given to live here under the sun. May we*

appreciate the covering that you offer us as we yield directly to your authority. May we appreciate the spiritual food and drink that you have made available. May we spend our time here on earth wisely. Amen.

Chapter Eight

An Evil Time

1 *Certainly I applied my heart unto all of this that I might declare all of this: that the righteous and the wise and their works are in the hand of God; no man knows either love or hatred by all that passes before them.*

According to our natural way of seeing things, we can love something that God does not love and hate something that God does not hate. But when the Lord comes into our life by the Holy Spirit, he changes our hearts and minds until we love what he loves and hate what he hates. If you don't believe that God hates certain things, just read the Scriptures. You'll find many things that God hates, things that he cannot accept in any way, shape, or form – things that the Bible says are an abomination unto the Lord.

What is an abomination?

An abomination is something that is not compatible with the presence of God. If we insist on keeping or fomenting an abomination, the Spirit of God will be grieved and withdraw from us. Eventually judgment will fall. This is what happened in Sodom and in Jerusalem.

> 2 *All things come alike to all: there is one event to the righteous and to the wicked; to the good and to the clean and to the unclean; to him that sacrifices and to him that does not sacrifice: as unto the good so unto the sinner; and unto him that swears as unto him that fears the oath.*

At the time that Solomon wrote this, Satan was still able to hold prisoner in Sheol (Hades in Greek) the souls of virtually everyone who died. In the parable of the rich man and Lazarus, Jesus described Hades as having two zones or compartments with a gulf between them, such that it was still possible for Lazarus and the rich man to have a conversation from one side to the other. Lazarus was in the arms of Abraham and the rich man was in torment (Luke 16:19-26).

This situation with Satan continued until the redemptive work of Jesus Christ was carried out, when he overcame the grave and took the keys of death and Hades from the Devil (Revelation 1:17-18). Jesus died for us and descended into Hades, into the lower parts of the earth; then he led captivity captive when he ascended on high with those who were his (Ephesians 4:8-10). When Jesus died for us and redeemed us, he opened the opportunity for the souls of Christians to go up to heaven instead of down to Sheol. None of this was clear at the time of Solomon who, even with extraordinary wisdom from God, could only discern the things that are done under the sun.

> 3 *This is an evil among all things that are done under the sun, that there is one event unto all; and also that the heart of the sons of men is full of evil, and madness is in their heart while they live, and after that they go to the dead.*

Sheol refers to the first death, which kills the body but not the soul. The word *Sheol* has been confused and mistranslated as "hell" in many English Bibles. The real hell, however, is the lake of fire, which is also described as the second death and is able to destroy both the body and the soul (Matthew 10:28). At the time of final judgment, Sheol or Hades must deliver up the dead who are there. In fact, even death and Hades will be cast into the lake of fire, along with whoever is not found written in the book of life (Revelation 20:11-15).

> 4 *For to him that is still among the living there is hope: for a living dog is better than a dead lion.*

> 5 *For the living know that they shall die, but the dead do not know anything; neither do they have any more reward, for their memory is placed into oblivion.*

This Scripture (and many others) rules out any possibility of Sheol having the properties of purgatory, such as being a place where souls expiate their sins before ascending to heaven. While we are still alive, there is hope regarding the eternal state of our soul. The dead do not know anything in the sense that they can no longer interact in any meaningful way with the living (this was the lament of the rich man). The dead can do nothing to gain a reward. Their memory is placed into oblivion. As bodiless souls in Sheol, they can do nothing to alter what they did or didn't do while they were alive.

> 6 *Even their love and their hatred and their envy is now perished; neither have they any more a portion in the age in any thing that is done under the sun.*

The door is completely closed upon the possibility of any interaction between the dead and anything that is done under the sun.

> 7 *Go, eat thy bread with joy and drink thy wine with a joyful heart that thy works might be acceptable unto God.*

If we are happy and joyful with the natural or spiritual provision God has provided for us, this will help ensure that our works might be acceptable to him. Paul describes not being thankful to God as being a first step into apostasy (Romans 1:21-32).

> 8 *Thy garments shall always be white, and thy head shall never lack ointment.*

If our works are acceptable unto God, our garments or covering will always be clean and white; we will be covered by the Holy Spirit (Revelation 19:8). If our head is

Jesus, the anointing of the Spirit (ointment) will never cease to flow unto all the members of the body of Christ.

> 9 *Live joyfully with the wife whom thou dost love all the days which thou art to live in this lake of vanity, which are given unto thee; all the days of thy vanity under the sun: for that is thy portion in this life, and in thy labour in which thou dost work under the sun.*

After all of his follies with women, Solomon finally came to the conclusion that it would be better to live joyfully with *the wife whom thou dost love* all the days of our natural life. It is best to be joyful, thankful, and faithful to the spouse that God provides for us. This is also true of our calling in God.

> 10 *Whatever thy hand finds to do, do it with all thy might, for there is no work nor device nor knowledge nor wisdom in Sheol, where thou goest.*

Sheol was basically set up as a prison for souls. At the time of Solomon, the Devil had the keys. Now that Jesus has taken the keys from him, Sheol remains a prison for the souls that do not go to heaven and are awaiting final judgment. Scripture implies that the time will soon come when the Devil will be locked up for *a thousand years* in what used to be his own prison (Revelation 20:1-3). During this time, Satan and his demons will no longer be able to interfere in the affairs of men under the sun.

> 11 *I returned and saw under the sun that the race is not to the swift, nor the battle to the*

> *strong, neither yet bread to the wise, nor yet riches to men of prudence, nor yet grace to men of eloquence; but time and chance happens to them all.*

Solomon took another hard look at this and saw that things are not as they first appear under the sun. Some times and seasons are very important and affect everyone. Chance affects everyone. When anyone makes a decision, it may generate a long series of consequences.

An important time looms on our modern horizon that is referred to in Scripture as the evil time or the evil day.

We have all been through difficult times when nothing seems to go right. In our younger days, we make mistakes through lack of experience, and we often pay the price for them, but we have the resilience of youth. As we grow older, we acquire more wisdom, but our bodies begin to betray us, and we must face the fact that the effects of old age will catch up to all of us. We have to learn to deal with these ordinary trials of life, but God can grant us the grace to pass each test.

But now, prior to the second coming of the Lord Jesus, an evil time is prophesied for the entire world. No one will escape. It will take place everywhere; it will affect every business, every city, and every town. Every nation will be shaken to the core. Everything that *can* be shaken on heaven and on earth *will* be shaken (Hebrews 12:25-29).

It will be clear that the race is not to the swift, nor the battle to the strong, neither bread to the wise, nor riches to men of prudence, nor grace to men of eloquence. Those who will enjoy victory at this time are those who have found shelter in the secret place of the most high under the wings of the Almighty (Psalm 91).

The United States considers itself the most powerful nation on the face of the earth, but it is facing serious problems; neither is it the only country to do so. Banks all around the world that were once solvent and powerful are shaking. Entire nations that were arrogant and full of bluster are being forced to their knees. Only that which has been accomplished by God will remain. Everything else will come down.

If our hope is in any of the things of this world, we will be deceived. But if we allow the Spirit of God to lead us, he will show us how to take the corruptible riches of this world and exchange them for true and incorruptible treasure in the heavenly realm.

I've heard it said that even though it's impossible to take any of the riches of this world with us when we die, it's possible to wire money on ahead into a heavenly bank account. The only way to accomplish this is to carefully obey the Lord and follow the leading and direction of the Holy Spirit regarding how we invest our time and resources here and now.

> 12 *For man also does not know his time: as the fishes that are taken in an evil net and as the birds that are caught in the snare, so are the sons of men snared in the evil time, when it falls suddenly upon them.*

An evil time is coming upon the sons of men who are

dwellers of the earth. Only the sons of God who have their real citizenship in heaven will survive. Paul wrote regarding this coming day of the Lord: *But of the times and the seasons, brethren, ye have no need that I write unto you. For ye know well that the day of the Lord shall come as a thief in the night. For when they shall say, Peace and safety; then sudden destruction shall come upon them, as travail upon a woman with child; and they shall not escape* (1 Thessalonians 5:1-3).

The only way to escape is to have a clean heart, and the only way to have a clean heart is to submit to the correction of Father God. Jesus said that (only) the pure in heart shall see God (Matthew 5:8).

> 13 *I have also seen this wisdom under the sun, which is important unto me:*

Solomon described virtually everything under the sun as vanity and vexation of spirit. This is one of the few times he mentions that something is important to him.

Why is this wisdom (described in the following verses) important to Solomon?

> 14 *There was a little city and few men within it; and a great king came against it and besieged it and built great bulwarks against it;*
>
> 15 *now there was found in it a poor wise man, and he by his wisdom delivered the city; yet no one remembered that same poor man.*

Who is the poor, forgotten wise man that delivered the little city?

The poor, obscure, forgotten wise man is certainly not King Solomon. Solomon was a rich, well-known wise man whose proverbial wisdom (confined most of his life to the realm under the sun) did *not* deliver his city. In fact, the seeds of apostasy sown by Solomon actually brought about his city's complete and total destruction. Jesus said that the one who is the least and is the servant of all is really the greatest in the Kingdom of God. It is the poor in spirit that will have the wisdom to save the little city.

What city is Solomon referring to?

The true people of God (in any age throughout human history) have always been a small remnant or *little city with few men within it*. Now, at the end of the age of grace, this metaphor is more relevant than ever. Those who stand for the truth are a small remnant in any venue of society.

Who is the great king that came against the little city?

In Scripture, the greatest of all kings is God (Psalm 47:2; Psalm 95:3). The remnant of the people of God has stood against the attacks of the world for six thousand years of recorded human history. Now, however, God is about to judge the earth by fire (2 Peter 3:7). God's people will be judged by his standard of absolute perfection. What will the people of God do when God himself besieges their *little city* (or the little kingdoms they have built for themselves in his name) and builds great ramparts against it?

How did the poor wise man deliver the city? Jesus said, *Blessed are the poor in spirit, for theirs is the kingdom of the heavens* (Matthew 5:3). We demonstrate the wisdom of the poor wise man when we let God deal with our pride and acknowledge that we can do nothing good without him; we should not even be building *little cities* on our own initiative. This is the wisdom of John the Baptist who said that he must decrease and Jesus Christ must increase (John 3:30).

The only way for any of us to survive the time of judgment coming upon the earth is for us to be hidden in Christ under the shadow of the wings of the Almighty. When God's mighty judgments fall upon the earth, Christ must *be* all and *in* all (Colossians 3:10-11). There is no margin of error. Our own merits, gifts, and accomplishments must be forgotten. Paul wrote that *Christ in you* is *the hope of glory* (Colossians 1:26-28). If we take no account of ourselves but are fully yielded to God, then when the world looks upon us, they will not see us but Christ.

> 16 *Then I said, Wisdom is better than strength: even though the poor man's knowledge is despised, and his words are not heard.*

The poor man's knowledge is despised today more than at any other time, and most will not hear his words. This may also be why only a *little city* is saved.

Jesus said: *Enter ye in at the narrow gate, for the way that leads to destruction is wide and spacious, and those who follow it are many; because narrow is the gate, and confined is the way which leads unto life, and there are few that find it* (Matthew 7:13-14).

Most of the time it is neither wise nor safe to follow the crowd.

> 17 *The words of wise men are heard in quiet more than the cry of him that rules among fools.*

In order for the words of wise men to be heard, there must be quiet. If we are part of the remnant of God but continue friendship with the world, the deafening noise around us will drown out the still, small voice of wisdom from God.

Who rules among fools?

The Devil rules in the midst of all the fools of this world.

> 18 *Wisdom is better than weapons of war, but one sinner destroys much good.*

Who is the one sinner that destroys much good? He is the old man, the man of sin in each and every one of us that must be vanquished, or much good will be destroyed.

Solomon found this to be true even in the midst of his many human accomplishments under the sun. The vast majority of the apparently good works of Solomon were destroyed. We are left with only a remnant of his accomplishments (such as this book of Ecclesiastes, The Book of the Preacher) because this demonstrates how God converted Solomon into a preacher with a special message for those who insist on doing "good" works with the gifts and abilities they have received from God without being willing to let go of the old, carnal man.

Jesus will return for a bride without spot or wrinkle

or any such thing. Not even one sinner will be among the body of the bride of Christ. The coming time, which is referred to in Scripture as Jacob's trouble or the great tribulation, will ensure that this is the case (Jeremiah 30:6-9).

Let us pray

Lord,
We ask that this great lesson from Solomon may remain clear to us so we need not repeat the same mistakes. May we understand that it is not worthwhile for us to seek the things of this world, not even food and clothing. May we seek first the kingdom of God and his righteousness and leave everything else in your hands. May your work be accomplished in us and through us. Amen.

Chapter Nine

Whosoever Moves the Stones ...

> 1 *Dead flies cause the ointment of the apothecary to send forth a stinking savour: likewise a small act of folly unto him that is esteemed for wisdom and honour.*

Dead flies in the ointment or anointing wreck everything. The wonderful fragrance of the anointing announces the proximity of the presence of the Lord. Conversely, even small acts of folly by those who are gifted and anointed by God soon create an unbearable stench.

> 2 *A wise man's heart is at his right hand, but a fool's heart at his left.*

Under normal conditions in the natural world, all of us humans are born with our hearts on our left side. Therefore, we are all fools in one way or another. The only wise man is Jesus Christ. The only way for us to become wise is to be born again in the life of Jesus Christ and come to maturity by the Spirit of God. The right hand is a symbol of authority and power linked to the throne of God. The resurrected, glorified Jesus Christ is seated at the right hand of the Father with all power and authority.

> 3 *Even when the fool walks by the way, he lacks prudence, and he says unto every one that he is a fool.*

For us to be wise and good, the Lord must order our steps (Psalm 37:23). The natural man (or woman) determines his own steps, and in so doing he broadcasts to everyone that he is a fool.

> 4 *If the spirit of the ruler rises up against thee, do not leave thy place; for meekness pacifies great sins.*

Many do not seem to be able to receive correction or even constructive criticism. They prefer to *leave their place* rather than be corrected. Jesus said, *Blessed are the meek, for they shall inherit the earth* (Matthew 5:5).

> 5 *There is another evil which I have seen under the sun, as an error which proceeds from the ruler:*

> 6 *Folly is set with great dignity, and the rich are seated in a low place.*

Jesus said that the time will come when some of those who are now first shall be last, and some of those who are now last shall be first (Luke 13:30).

> 7 *I saw slaves upon horses, and princes walking as slaves upon the earth.*

In this present time of training and formation, God has many of his sons (princes) walking as servants (slaves) upon the earth. Those who are receiving the necessary training to receive the true inheritance may not be riding on "horses" right now. They are walking with the Lord in the midst of many trials and tribulations.

> 8 *He that digs a pit will fall into it, and whosoever breaks a hedge, a serpent shall bite him.*

Many people dig pits for others to fall into. In fact, the entire world economy is one big pit that such people have been digging for quite some time. Today, by means of deceptive central monetary policy, many are *breaking down hedges* and pilfering that which does not belong to them. This is finally catching up to them, however, and the *serpent* is about to bite.

For the past hundred years or so, the economic policy of many governments has been greatly influenced by the British economist John Maynard Keynes, who taught that it is not necessary to back up hard currency with something of real value. Keynes taught that in order to stimulate economies in times of recession, depression, or contraction, governments could embark on deficit spending and attempt to literally make money out of nothing.

This, however, will only work on short or medium time frames. Over the long haul, it's a disaster. Keynes also famously said, "Capitalism is the astounding belief that the most wickedest of men will do the most wickedest of things for the greatest good of everyone."

> 9 *Whosoever moves the stones shall have tribulation along with it, and he that cuts the firewood shall be endangered by it.*

What does it mean to *move the stones*?

It means to move the established laws, rules, or boundaries, such as the Ten Commandments written by God upon tablets of stone (Exodus 24:12). It means to use underhanded tactics and change equitable weights and measures. Modern economics and markets are full of this behavior. Modern society even wants to move established moral boundaries that have been "set in stone" for centuries, regarding things like gender and marriage. Those who attempt to foist such aberrations on society shall not escape tribulation along with what they are doing.

Who is *he that cuts the firewood*? Dead wood symbolizes dead works. All those who are furthering the wrong policies (those who are moving the stones) will eventually be endangered by all the *firewood* that they have cut, when their works are judged by fire.

> 10 *If the iron is blunt, and he does not whet the edge, then he must put forth more strength, but the advantages of wisdom excel.*

Iron is also a symbol of the law. The laws of man are blunt and therefore do not cut well. They are not capable of cutting out the dead works of man, even when more *strength* is applied. One needs true wisdom to rightly apply the law of God.

11 *If the serpent bites without being enchanted, then the babbler is no more.*

The world is full of those who pay lip service to God but seek the things of this world. Such people are under the control of the ancient serpent, the Devil. Therefore, they must attempt to charm or to enchant the serpent, but sooner or later, it will bite them. The words of these fools will then be revealed as useless babble or confusion.

12 *The words from the mouth of the wise man are grace, but the lips of the fool will swallow up himself.*

13 *The beginning of the words of his mouth is foolishness, and the end of his talk is mischievous madness.*

Grace relates to the power of God to do for us what we are unable to do for ourselves. Those who are destitute of the grace of God can produce nothing but mischievous madness.

14 *The fool multiplies words and says, Man cannot tell what shall be, and what shall be after him, who can tell him?*

People don't know where they're going; they don't know what will happen in the future; they aren't even able to make simple projections into the future that jibe with reality, yet they want to be in charge. They can't even take an accurate poll due to all the hidden factors that must be tweaked plus the fact that a growing percentage of those polled, for one reason or another, do not answer truthfully.

> 15 *The labour of the foolish wearies all of them because they do not know how to go to the city.*

The natural man becomes fatigued because he is never able to arrive at the proper destination. He may have lofty goals and ambitions for himself and for society, but without God's guidance, he is unable to properly implement them. On the other hand, Jesus said that his yoke is easy and his burden is light. If we allow Jesus to do his work in and through us, we will be energized and filled with joy.

> 16 *Woe to thee, O land, when thy king is a child, and thy princes banquet in the morning!*

When the leader is immature, everything goes wrong. When the immature win the election or come into power, they and their followers *banquet in the morning* and divvy up the spoils. Like spoiled children, they think only of their own desires. They never give a thought to serving the people, much less serving God.

> 17 *Blessed art thou, O land, when thy king is the son of nobles, and thy princes eat in due season for strength, and not for drunkenness!*

Starting in the Old Testament, the Scriptures describe two basic classes of people in the world. This does not necessarily line up exactly with the rich versus the poor, as many believe today. People in Scripture are divided between the nobles (who are born free) and those who are not of noble birth (essentially servants or slaves).

In the highest sense, those who are born again into the life of the Lord Jesus Christ are no longer servants or slaves to the world, the flesh, and the Devil. Looked at from this perspective, how many of our world leaders are truly of noble birth? How many of our *princes eat in due season for strength and not for drunkenness*? Where are the selfless patriots who are willing to sacrifice for the people and for the nation?

> 18 *By much slothfulness the building decays, and through idleness of the hands the rain drips throughout the house.*

Those who are slaves to the flesh, the world, and the Devil never take timely initiative to protect society. Their values are such that they passively oversee the decay of western civilization, while corruption and moral hazard permeate the whole structure of our civilization until the entire world is endangered.

> 19 *The banquet is made for pleasure, and wine makes merry; but money answers all things.*

There are two basic types of wine and therefore two very different banquets. Wine, as a symbol of life, can represent our old corrupt life in Adam or the incorruptible new life that we can only find in Jesus Christ. Even though it is true that money answers all things, it is also true that the love of money is the root of all evil (1 Timothy 6:10). It is much better to take Jesus' advice and seek first the kingdom of God and his righteousness, so that he may then add unto us everything else that we need (Matthew 6:33).

> 20 *Do not curse the king, not even in thy thought; and do not curse the rich even in the secret place of thy bedchamber; for the birds of the air shall carry the voice, and those who have wings shall tell the matter.*

This is the advice of King Solomon inspired by the Spirit of God, but only after having learned many lessons the hard way.

Those who are dedicated to laziness and pleasure will not end well. Those who curse others for their problems while they inebriate themselves on the wine of their own corrupt lives will watch their houses decay under the steady drip of the corruption that emanates from their own hearts and seeps through the roof until the whole structure collapses.

It is all too easy to blame others for problems that in reality have a lot to do with the status of our own hearts.

Those who live in darkness always tend to be motivated primarily by fear of man and of circumstances. They covet the wrong things and operate according to the corrupt ways of this world while attempting to charm or enchant the serpent in order to get away with their rotten schemes.

The Lord says that if we forsake the corruption of this world to walk with him, we will not have to enchant serpents. Instead, we will be able to take them away before they can harm us (Mark 16:18). If we humble ourselves and submit to the mighty hand of God, we will be able to resist the Devil, and he will flee from us (James 4:7). Then no weapon formed against us will prosper (Isaiah

54:17). Whatever our enemies unjustly attempt to do to us will come back upon their own heads (Revelation 11:5).

However, similar to Solomon during much of his life, many people are struggling in the midst of moral defeat because they failed to submit to the discipline and correction of God the Father early in their lives.

Let us pray

Lord,
Thank you for the clarity of your word that we may be guided by your light through all of the circumstances around us. May the light of your truth illuminate our hearts and displace all shadows so you may work through us.
Amen.

Chapter Ten

Cast Thy Bread Upon the Waters

> 1 *Cast thy bread upon the waters, for thou shalt find it after many days.*

Scripture describes a *great whore that sits upon many waters* (Revelation 17:1). In this case, as with many times in Scripture when the sea of lost humanity is mentioned, the waters refer to people. Our *bread* is the provision that we have received from God (natural and spiritual). It is the will of God that we share what we have with others, so that the light of our example will cause others to see our good works and glorify our Father who is in the heavens (Matthew 5:16).

> 2 *Give a portion to seven and even to eight, for thou dost not know what evil shall come upon the earth.*

We are to give generously to as many as possible. Many

times in history, there have been evil days upon the earth, and the end time is described as an evil day for many. Jesus said, *Blessed are the merciful, for they shall obtain mercy* (Matthew 5:7).

> 3 *If the clouds are full of rain, they shall empty themselves upon the earth; and if the tree falls toward the south or toward the north, in the place where the tree falls, there it shall remain.*

If we are citizens of the heavenly realm, identified with the *clouds*, God can use us as a source of blessing to reach out to those who are lost upon the earth. Scripture also states that the life of men can be like a tree (Deuteronomy 20:19). By the end of our life here upon the earth, the eternal state of our soul will be defined. Each *tree* will fall either to the *north* or the *south*, where it will remain. Each person will either be saved or lost. There is no intermediate option.

> 4 *He that observes the wind shall not sow, and he that regards the clouds shall not reap.*

If we get distracted by the conditions around us and do not keep our eyes upon the Lord, we will miss opportunity after opportunity to *sow*. Many Christians are so obsessed with *regarding the clouds*, observing all the trouble around them, and thinking they will soon be raptured off to heaven that they are unable or unwilling to participate in reaping the harvest for the kingdom of God, but this harvest must be gathered here upon the earth.

> 5 *As thou dost not know what is the way of*

> *the spirit nor how the bones grow in the womb of her that is with child, even so thou dost not know the works of God who makes all.*

None of us know what the way of the spirit is. God is constantly birthing new things. He is busy working on a new creation. Each and every person born again by the Spirit of God is part of the works of God. God promises to birth an entire nation in one day, in the day of the Lord (Isaiah 66:7-8). That day is now upon us.

> 6 *In the morning sow thy seed, and in the evening withhold not thine hand; for thou knowest not which shall prosper, either this or that or whether they both shall be equally good.*

Paul encouraged Timothy to be ready in season and out of season (2 Timothy 4:2). We must be ready to plant the word of God whenever the Holy Spirit prompts us.

> 7 *Truly the light is sweet, and a pleasant thing it is for the eyes to behold the sun,*

> 8 *but if a man lives many years and rejoices in them all; yet if afterwards he remembers the days of darkness, for they shall be many, he shall say that everything that shall have happened to him is vanity.*

In the realm under the sun, symbolized by the outer court of the temple, the light of the sun is sweet and pleasant to behold. We must bear in mind, however, that the darkness of night dominates this realm half of the time. This realm under the sun of this world has many trials, tribulations, and evils. If we use our time under the sun wisely, seek God early, cast our bread upon the waters, and sow our seed in the morning and in the evening, then we have the hope of coming to maturity, bearing good and wholesome fruit for the kingdom of God, and entering the realm of eternity with great joy at the time of the final judgment.

> 9 *Rejoice, O young man, in thy youth, and let thy heart cheer thee in the days of thy youth and walk in the ways of thine heart and in the sight of thine eyes; but know thou, that for all these things God will bring thee into judgment.*

When we try out our own "good" ideas and leaven the things of God according to the ways of our hearts in the sight of our eyes, thinking that we are doing him a favor, God allows us to proceed. We may rejoice in our youth and let our hearts cheer us, but God will also bring us into judgment for all of these things. He will make the final decision regarding what is good and what is evil. He will review what we have planted and what we have harvested.

> 10 *Therefore remove sorrow from thy heart and put away evil from thy flesh, for childhood and youth are vanity.*

The way to remove sorrow from our hearts and put away evil from our flesh is to come to maturity in Christ. Spiritual childhood, symbolized by the outer court of the temple under the sun, is vanity – so is spiritual youth, symbolized by the Holy Place of priestly ministry.

(Remember that now, in the age of the church, we are in the priesthood of all born-again believers.) If we are the seed that God desires to plant in the lives of those around us, then we must come to maturity in order to be viable (Matthew 13:37-43).

Why?

The only way to bear good and lasting fruit is to come to maturity (perfection in Hebrew). In nature, the viable seed is in the mature fruit. As believers, coming to maturity is the only way to come into the fullness of the life of Christ. It is the only way to completely put away the evil from our flesh. The Lord Jesus Christ is mature (perfect), and he desires to rule and to reign in our hearts.

Everything that man comes up with apart from God is vanity. Apart from God, man can accomplish nothing of eternal value. God seeks to work in and through us. He desires a people who have come to maturity (perfection) by completely surrendering to Jesus Christ and are therefore moved by him. Then God will multiply his people, and they will dominate the earth, not through violence, intimidation, and coercion, but through the all-encompassing love of God.

The apostle Paul wrote: *For though we walk in the flesh, we do not war after the flesh (For the weapons of our warfare are not carnal, but mighty through God for the destruction of strong holds), casting down reasonings and every high thing that exalts itself against the knowledge of God and leading captive every thought into the obedience of the Christ and having a readiness to avenge all disobedience, when your obedience is fulfilled* (2 Corinthians 10:3-6).

Jesus said simply, *Be ye therefore perfect, even as your Father who is in the heavens is perfect* (Matthew 5:48).

Jesus will return for a bride *without spot or wrinkle or any such thing* (Ephesians 5:27). The corporate bride of Christ is a congregation that will not walk in the foolishness and vanity of immature childhood or youth.

Ecclesiastes 12

> 1 *Remember now thy Creator in the days of thy youth while the evil days do not come nor the years draw near when thou shalt say, I have no pleasure in them;*

All of us are on a time line. We advance into old age and die. Isaiah wrote that the same is true about the earth. In Scripture, the earth can represent the people of God. The age of the church, the age of grace, is also coming to an end. At the time of the end, there shall be evil days in which all the sinners and ungodly who dwell upon the earth shall definitely have no pleasure in them. The world is obviously now in those days.

> *Lift up your eyes to the heavens, and look upon the earth beneath; for the heavens shall vanish away like smoke, and the earth shall wax old like a garment, and those that dwell therein shall perish in like manner; but my saving health shall be for ever, and my righteousness shall never perish* (Isaiah 51:6).

If we are born again by the Spirit of God into the life of Jesus Christ, then the Jerusalem of above is the mother of us all (Galatians 4:26). Then we are citizens of heaven even while we continue to walk uprightly upon this earth in the overcoming power of the Holy Spirit. Then we will not have to fear the righteous judgments of God upon the earth, because he never destroys the righteous along with the wicked (Genesis 18:23-32).

> 1 *Remember now thy Creator in the days of thy youth while the evil days do not come nor the years draw near when thou shalt say, I have no pleasure in them;*
>
> 2 *before the sun and the light and the moon and the stars are darkened and the clouds return after the rain:*

The time will soon come when the realm under the sun will be judged and everyone will reap what they have sown (Galatians 6:7-10). The light of this world will go out. The moon, symbolizing the people of God (Israel and the church), will also be darkened for those who have been reflecting the light of the sun of this world instead of the light of God. The stars, symbolic of those who have gifts and ministries from God, will also be darkened because the time for this will be ended. The lamps of the foolish virgins will go out. Only those who are properly joined to the Lord Jesus will be hid in Christ. Joel wrote concerning that day: *The sun and the moon shall be darkened, and the stars shall withdraw their shining. The LORD also shall roar out of Zion and utter his voice from Jerusalem; and the heavens and the earth shall shake; but the LORD will be the hope of his people and the strength of the sons of Israel* (Joel 3:15-16).

Jesus discussed the same thing with his disciples, telling them, *Immediately after the tribulation of those days shall the sun be darkened, and the moon shall not give her light, and the stars shall fall from the heaven, and the powers of the heavens shall be shaken* (Matthew 24:29).

Mark recalls that discussion in these words: *But in those days after that affliction, the sun shall darken, and the moon shall not give her light, and the stars shall fall from heaven, and the powers that are in the heavens shall be shaken. And then shall they see the Son of man coming in the clouds with great power and glory* (Mark 13:24-26).

This is when, according to the Preacher, *the clouds return after the rain*. This time is closely connected to the return of Jesus Christ.

> 2 *before the sun and the light and the moon*
> *and the stars are darkened and the clouds*
> *return after the rain:*
>
> 3 *In the day when the keepers of the house*
> *shall tremble and the strong men shall bow*
> *themselves and the grinders cease because*
> *they are few and those that look out of the*
> *windows are darkened;*

Who are *the keepers of the house*?

Ezekiel describes them as the priests that led Israel astray. They will not be granted access to minister in the presence of the Lord (Ezekiel 44:10-14). Jesus describes them as hypocrites who shut up the kingdom of the heavens in front of men and neither go in themselves nor allow others who are entering to go in (Matthew 23:13).

Who are *the strong men*?

They are those who try to please God by attempting to keep his commandments in their own strength instead of having the indwelling power and presence of the Holy Spirit.

Who are *the grinders*?

They were slaves who would power the millstone to grind the grain. Many leaders and ministers work for days to grind out their Sunday morning message while they continue to be slaves to the flesh, the world, and ultimately the Devil. Where the Spirit of the Lord is, there is liberty, and the word of God flows freely (2 Corinthians 3:17).

Who are *those that look out of the windows* that shall be darkened?

This refers to those who have enclosed themselves in man-made fortresses of religion.

> 4 *and the doors outside shall be shut because the voice of the grinder is low, and he shall rise up at the voice of the bird and all the daughters of song shall be humbled;*

The voice of the grinder is so low in many religious institutions that they eventually shut their doors. Many cathedrals and church buildings are shuttered or in ruins or have become virtual museums. This trend has dominated much of Europe, and North America is not far behind. The prophet Zephaniah had this to say: *both the cormorant and the bittern shall lodge in her thresholds; their voice shall sing in the windows; desolation shall be in the gates: for her cedar work shall be uncovered* (Zephaniah 2:14). The *cedar work* is the dead works of humanistic religion that shall be exposed for what they are.

Who are *the daughters of song*?

They are the cantors of the temple. Here is a parallel passage: *And the cantors of the temple shall howl in that day, said the Lord GOD; there shall be many dead bodies in every place; they shall cast them forth with silence* (Amos 8:3).

The Preacher continues:

> 5 *when they shall also be afraid of that which is high, and fears shall be in the way, and the almond tree shall flourish, and the grasshopper shall be a burden, and appetite shall fail: because man goes to the home of his age, and the mourners shall go about in the streets;*

Why shall they *be afraid of that which is high*?

The same scene is described by the apostle John: *And I saw when he had opened the sixth seal, and, behold, there was a great earthquake; and the sun became black as sackcloth of hair, and the moon became as blood, and the stars of heaven fell upon the earth, even as a fig tree casts her figs, when she is shaken of a mighty wind. And the heaven departed as a scroll when it is rolled together; and every mountain and island were moved out of their places.*

And the kings of the earth and the princes and the rich and the captains and the strong and every slave and every free man hid themselves in the caves and among the rocks of the mountains and said to the mountains and to the rocks, Fall on us and hide us from the face of him that is seated upon the throne and from the wrath of the Lamb; for the great day of his wrath is come, and who shall be able to stand before him? (Revelation 6:12-17).

What is *the almond tree* that shall flourish?

The rod of Aaron blossomed overnight and bore almonds, thus proving who was the high priest approved by God (Numbers 17:8). Jesus is *named by God high priest after the order of Melchisedec* (Hebrews 5:10). At the imminent return of Jesus Christ, the almond tree of the rod of his righteous judgments shall flourish.

What is the *grasshopper* or locust that shall be a burden, and what *appetite shall fail*?

Locusts were one of the plagues of Egypt. The prophet Joel described them as being part of the judgments of the day of the Lord (Joel 1:4), and the apostle John gives a vivid description of locusts that will sting those *who do not have the seal of God in their foreheads* (Revelation 9:3-6).

The three stages to the word of God are symbolized in one of Jesus' parables as being first the blade (or grass), then the flower, and then the mature grain (Mark 4:28). The natural man, on the other hand, is compared in Scripture to a beast that eats grass (Daniel 4:16, 25; Psalm 73:22; Ecclesiastes 3:19). In the day of the Lord, when God sends in the *locusts*, the provision for those carnal Christians who would fatten themselves on the letter of the word like cows in a pasture will be removed, and therefore their *appetite shall fail.*

Where is *the home of his age* for the natural man?

His home is Sheol (Hades), the first death, which can kill the body but not the soul (Matthew 10:28). In Scripture, this is very distinct from the second death, which is the lake of fire (the real hell), prepared for the final judgment of the Devil and his followers. At the final judgment, Hades must give up her dead so they may be judged (Revelation 20:13-14).

Prior to Jesus' work of redemption (by his sinless life, death, and resurrection), Satan held the souls of virtually everyone who had died, including Abraham and the patriarchs, in Hades or Sheol, known as the bottomless pit or abyss. The parable of the rich man and Lazarus demonstrates that at that time Hades had two compartments with a great gulf between them, but Abraham and Lazarus on one side could communicate with the rich man who was in torment on the other side (Luke 16:22-26).

After his death, Jesus descended into Hades, the first death (not into the lake of fire, which is the second death) and led captivity captive by freeing those who were his and ascending on high (Ephesians 4:8-10). Jesus took the keys to Hades from the Devil (Revelation 1:18). After the return of Jesus and immediately prior to his reign on earth for a thousand years with those who take part in the first resurrection, the Devil will be bound in that same bottomless pit for a thousand years (Revelation 20:1-3).

Why will the *mourners* go about in the streets?

When Jesus returns, he will cleanse his own house first. This is what he warned will happen: *But and if that slave shall say in his heart, My lord delays his coming, and shall begin to beat the menslaves and maids and to eat and drink and to be drunken, the lord of that slave will come in a day when he does not look for him and at an hour when he is not aware and will cut him off and will appoint him his portion with the unfaithful* (Luke 12:45-46).

Finishing his sermon and speaking under the anointing of the Holy Spirit, Solomon is not only preaching to all of the young people who would be born over the next three thousand years, he is giving a prophetic warning and a detailed symbolic picture of what will happen immediately prior to and at the second coming of the Lord Jesus Christ.

> 5 *when they shall also be afraid of that which is high, and fears shall be in the way, and the almond tree shall flourish, and the grasshopper shall be a burden, and appetite shall fail: because man goes to the home of his age, and the mourners shall go about in the streets;*
>
> 6 *before the silver chain is broken, and the golden bowl is broken, and the pitcher is*

broken at the fountain, and the wheel is broken at the cistern;

What is the *silver chain*?

After all the idolatry that Solomon involved himself in with his pagan wives, he knew very well what silver chains could be used for. Scripture can shed some light on this: *To whom then will ye liken God? or what likeness will ye compare unto him? The workman prepares the graven image, and the goldsmith spreads it over with gold and casts silver chains* (Isaiah 40:18-19).

Silver symbolizes redemption, but it can also become tarnished; this is why we are exhorted to take due diligence to make our calling and election sure (2 Peter 1:10). A chain can symbolize bondage, which was why pagan idols had silver chains. No matter which of its many forms it takes, idolatry eventually ends in bondage. As Samuel told King Saul, *rebellion is the sin of witchcraft, and to break the word of the Lord is iniquity and idolatry* (1 Samuel 15:23).

Solomon found out the hard way that sooner or later the *silver chain* will break and the idols will not be able to protect anyone.

What is the *golden bowl*?

The apostle John saw seven golden vials full of the wrath of God (Revelation 15:7). The word *vials* implies that these were enclosed bowls that had to be broken for the final judgments of God to be poured out upon the earth. Once the golden bowl is broken, there is no further opportunity for rebellious workers of iniquity to rectify their behavior.

What is the *pitcher* that *is broken at the fountain*?

Pitchers were mainly used to draw water from a well or fountain (Genesis 24:18-20). Jesus told the woman at the well that he could give her living water. If the pitcher is broken at the fountain, this means that the person has sinned away his day of grace, and his opportunity is gone. This is what happened with Judas: when he finally attempted to repent, it was too late.

What is the *wheel* that *is broken at the cistern*?

A cistern is a deep pit or well, and the wheel was the pulley that enabled the thirsty person to use a long rope to access the water. If the wheel is broken, access to the water that is necessary for life is gone.

> *7 and the dust returns to the earth as it was before and the spirit returns unto God who gave it.*

God created man from the dust of the earth and breathed into his nostrils the breath of life (Genesis 2:7). The word *breath* is the same as the word *spirit* in Hebrew. We have a limited amount of time here under the sun, and we must use it wisely. Otherwise, we will return to the dust of the earth, and the spirit (or breath) that was in us will return unto God. For *it is appointed unto men to die once, and after this the judgment* (Hebrews 9:27). Whether the tree falls to the north or to the south, where it has fallen is where it will remain.

> 8 *Vanity of vanities, saith the preacher, all is vanity.*
>
> 9 *And the wiser the preacher became that much more did he teach wisdom to the people, causing them to listen and to search things out, and he composed many proverbs.*
>
> 10 *The preacher sought to find willing words and upright writings, even words of truth.*

The real preacher behind all of this is the Lord. Solomon was inspired by the Spirit of God to write this sermon, and Scripture states unequivocally that *the Lord is the Spirit* (2 Corinthians 3:17).

> 11 *The words of the wise are as goads and as nails hammered into place, those of the teachers of the congregations, who are placed under one Shepherd.*

The Lord Jesus Christ is the one Shepherd, and all the teachers of his congregations are placed under his authority and supervision.

> 12 *My son, in addition to this, be admonished: of making books there is no end, and much study is a weariness of the flesh.*
>
> 13 *The conclusion of the entire sermon is heard: Fear God and keep his commandments, for this is the whole happiness of man.*
>
> 14 *For God shall bring every work to*

judgment with every secret thing, whether it is good or whether it is evil.

Let us pray

Lord,
We ask for greater clarity for you to illuminate our hearts. May we have the right focus. May your cleansing work in our hearts clear up our vision, so we may see things from your perspective. May we see your goals. May we desire to walk in your ways. May we arrive victorious at the finish line of the race that is set before us without turning aside after the things of this world. Amen.

Afterword

The Lord is touching people all over the world and waking them up to an awareness of his presence. This has been happening in the remote jungles and mountains of Colombia in the midst of the upheaval of a civil war that has been going on for more than fifty-two years.

My octogenarian friend, Buddy Cobb, shared some thoughts at a convention in the eastern department of Caqueta, after being absent from the region for almost twenty-six years due to all the violence. He said:

"We're getting closer and closer to the time when the Lord will return. Much of the church is anxiously awaiting the second coming of Jesus, but Jesus is waiting for his people to return to him.

"The people of God want the Lord to solve their problems by taking them away to be with him, but God says that if we return unto him, he will return unto us.

"Jesus spoke about this in parables. One was about the ten virgins. They all had lamps, but at the time of the return of the bridegroom all of the virgins were asleep. The foolish virgins were asleep and so were the wise ones. When they all awakened from their slumber, the foolish ones discovered that their lamps were going out for lack of oil. While they sought the necessary oil, the bridegroom came, and only the wise were able to enter in."

Many among the people of God, even those who could be typed as "wise" virgins, are spiritually asleep and need to be awakened.

In Jesus' parable, *all* the virgins fell asleep (Matthew 25:1-5). Most of the people of God (in the congregations of the church and in Israel) are also asleep in the sense that they are completely unaware of the lateness of the hour and the urgency of the situation. The hour is now upon us when many will be rudely awakened from their spiritual slumber. Only those with a direct, personal relationship with the source of the oil (anointing) will be able to enter in to the fullness of the purposes of God as the return of Jesus becomes imminent.

Buddy also remarked, "Many Christians today are like Christmas trees. There's a lot of glitter, lights, and gifts, but they have a serious problem. Their tree is cut and has no roots. They'll never produce good fruit."

Jesus said that he is the vine and we are the branches. Without him we can do nothing. As we abide in him, we will bear good fruit (John 15:1-8).

Appearances can be very deceptive. This is not about religious vocabulary, ritual, or even gifts. If we're not connected to Jesus, we will never produce the fruit of the Holy Spirit, which is the fruit of his righteousness.

Jesus said that we shall know them *by their fruits* (Matthew 7:20).

When he returns, he will deal with those who are producing evil fruit in his name. When he was here the first time, Jesus cursed the fig tree that had no fruit. This time he will judge those who are Christians in name only, who are not bearing good fruit or whose fruit is bitter.

As Solomon says, *I went down into the garden of nuts to see the fruits of the valley, and to see whether the vines flourished, and the pomegranates budded. Or ever I was aware, my soul made me return like the chariots of Amminadib* (Song of Solomon 6:11-12).

When Jesus knows that his bride is at the peak of her beauty, without spot or wrinkle or any such thing and producing perfect fruit, he will return.

Now is the time to return unto the Lord and seek him with our whole heart.

Russell Martin Stendal

La Havana

March 2016

Meet the Author

Russell Stendal, a former hostage of Colombian rebels, is a lifelong missionary to that same group in the jungles of Colombia. He is an influential friend to military and government leaders in Colombia, Cuba, Mexico, Venezuela, and the United States. Russell's ministry shares the gospel via twelve radio stations, hundreds of thousands of Bibles, books, and movies distributed through airplane parachute drops, and numerous speaking engagements for groups of leaders, prisoners, and individuals. Russell goes wherever the Lord leads, whether it's to speak with a president or to go deep into the jungle to help an individual in trouble. He has witnessed thousands commit their lives to Christ.

Connect with the Author

Website: www.cpcsociety.ca
Newsletter Signup: www.anekopress.com/stendal-newsletter

Russell and his coworkers have built dozens of radio stations in Latin America that concentrate a clear message on remote and dangerous areas where persecution of Christians is rampant. More than 120,000 Galcom solar-powered radios have been deployed to those being discipled. Most of the programming is in Spanish, but they also transmit in almost a dozen native languages where a great move of God is presently taking place. Russell preaches through the Bible, a chapter or so per message. More than 1,000 messages have been recorded and aired repeatedly. The chapters of this book are samples of these messages preached on the radio in the Colombian war zone about ten years ago. The key website is www.fuerzadepaz.com. Pray for Russell and his team as they expand Spanish-language radio coverage into places like Cuba, Venezuela, Mexico, and Central America.

Plans are in the works for new stations broadcasting in English that will provide coverage into Africa (where there are over 300 million English speakers) and possibly even into Asia and the Middle East. The first stage, as the programming is refined, will be Internet radio. After that, we want to begin shortwave radio transmission and distribution of Galcom radios in Africa and elsewhere as God opens the doors. The new radios have digital audio Bibles on board, and the goal is to move in the direction of digital shortwave transmissions within the next few years.

Connect with Russell's Ministry

Website

www.cpcsociety.ca

Receive newsletter updates

http://goo.gl/amBsCD

Buy books

http://amzn.to/1nPLcNL

40706054R00089

Made in the USA
Middletown, DE
20 February 2017